Intercultural Constitutionalism

This book argues that the effective protection of fundamental rights in a contemporary, multicultural society requires not only tolerance and respect for others, but also an ethics of reciprocity and a pursuit of dialogue between different cultures of human rights. Nowadays, all cultures tend to claim an equitable arrangement that can be articulated in the terms of fundamental rights and in the multicultural organization of the State. Starting from the premise that every culture is and always was intercultural, this book elaborates a new, and more fundamentally, pluralist view of the relationship between rights and cultural identity. No culture is pure; from the perspective of an irreducible cultural contamination, this book argues, it is possible to formulate constitutional idea of diversity that is properly intercultural. This concept of intercultural constitutionalism is not, then, based on abstract principles, nor is it bound to any particular cultural norm. Rather, intercultural constitutionalism allows the interpretation of rights, rules and legal principles, which are established in different contexts.

Salvatore Bonfiglio is Professor of Comparative Public Law at the Department of Political Studies of Roma Tre University and Director of the Multimedia Laboratory of Comparative Law. He is also Director of the online scientific period *Democracy and Security Review*.

Intercultural Constitutionalism

From Human Rights Colonialism
to a New Constitutional Theory
of Fundamental Rights

Salvatore Bonfiglio

Routledge
Taylor & Francis Group
a GlassHouse Book

First published 2019
by Routledge
2 Park Square, Milton Park, Abingdon, Oxon OX14 4RN

and by Routledge
52 Vanderbilt Avenue, New York, NY 10017

First issued in paperback 2020

a GlassHouse book
Routledge is an imprint of the Taylor & Francis Group, an informa business

British Library Cataloguing-in-Publication Data
A catalogue record for this book is available from the British
Library

Library of Congress Cataloging-in-Publication Data
Names: Bonfiglio, Salvatore.
Title: Intercultural constitutionalism : from human rights
    colonialism to a new constitutional theory of fundamental rights /
Salvatore Bonfiglio.
Description: New York, NY : Routledge, 2019. | Includes
    bibliographical references and index.
Identifiers: LCCN 2018034623 | ISBN 9781138393905 (hbk)
Subjects: LCSH: Civil rights. | Human rights. | Cultural pluralism. |
    Constitutional law.
Classification: LCC K3240 .B665 2019 | DDC 342.08/5—dc23
LC record available at https://lccn.loc.gov/2018034623

ISBN 13: 978-0-367-67042-9 (pbk)
ISBN 13: 978-1-138-39390-5 (hbk)

Typeset in Times New Roman by Apex
CoVantage, LLC

To my existing grandchildren . . . and those
still to come

Contents

Preface

So why did I write this book? Well, it is down to a belief that the history, theory and protection of fundamental rights truly matter – for three major reasons. Firstly, the study of the historical roots and philosophical and legal bases of fundamental rights confirms the need to overcome the generic universality of human rights rhetoric. Secondly, the progressive recognition of fundamental rights exemplifies some typical and significant stages of contemporary constitutionalism. Thirdly, work in this area fuels the demand for an effective protection of fundamental rights in contemporary, multicultural societies.

Constitutionalism and the normative 'force' of its principles confront the challenges posed not only by the current multicultural phenomenon, largely affected by growing migration flows, but also by processes within the framework of economic globalization, commercialization and the violation of individual and collective rights.

All too often, within this complex international reality, the rules of the main economic actors, formalized as independent, sectoral 'constitutions' above the control of public authorities or citizens, means that constitutional principles and values – such as human dignity and the principles of equality, representation and democratic participation – become undermined. So ironically, the confirmation of these sectoral dynamics threatens the very concept of constitutionalism itself, which must remain unified and focused on its clear, practical purpose: the recognition of fundamental rights and their protection.

For the protection of fundamental rights to actually be effective, it cannot be fragmented, or broken up into different sectors. For protection to be effective, what is needed is: (a) a reasonable balance between diverse, and even opposing, requirements that must be constitutionally recognized and protected in a unitary, principle-based framework; (b) a (vertical and horizontal) separation of powers; (c) a broad system of constitutional guarantees, all with the aim of sustaining constitutional order (such as the provision for a special, constitutional revision procedure that sets down both formal and material limits to the revision itself: principles and fundamental rights).

Placing the importance of economic priorities above law and politics, coupled with the fact of unstoppable and increasing migration, has raised questions about the structure of democratic states and the very science of constitutional law. This brings up old and new problems of social cohesion. Fundamental constitutional principles, starting with freedom, equality and solidarity, do not need to be entirely abandoned – but they do need a significant re-reading, from an intercultural perspective, to counteract ideological fanaticism and religious extremism actions, which have absolutely no relation to politics and religion.

In fact, what multicultural societies need is a reinterpretation of constitutional principles, in order to promote social cohesion, including the extension of fundamental rights to 'non-citizens'. This is about recognizing not only the moral but also the legal nature of human dignity, in a statute of fundamental individual rights. Only when we start to put value in the connection between dignity and rights can we destroy the traditional notion of citizenship, redefining its meaning in more inclusive terms, that is, as a fundamental rights citizenship. Moreover, it is crucial that, beyond that extension of a person's fundamental rights, we offer a recognition of new individual and collective rights. That is just what this work aims do – to integrate the 'liberal multiculturalism' perspective, firmly anchored in individual rights, with the 'democratic multiculturalism' perspective, that values cultural and social differences in the field of fundamental rights and principles, as well as in political and institutional frameworks.

Salvatore Bonfiglio
Rome, May 2016

Part I

Fundamental rights in the light of their evolution

1 Fundamental rights

Amidst "Nature" and "History"

1.1 Introduction

The year 2015 was a very important one. Why? Because it saw the celebration of the 800th anniversary of the Magna Carta of 1215. It was a key celebration, recalling as it did the significance of the first – or at least the most well-known[1] – constitutional document of the pre-modern era, setting in motion the whole process of positive fundamental rights in Europe.[2]

Now, from a non-Eurocentric research perspective, it's important to recall that, in other cultural contexts, codes or charters were written for the rationalization of fundamental rights, in some cases taking on the character of proto-constitutions. Take, for instance, the constitution or charter of Medina conceived by Muhammad in the year 622, which determined several rights and responsibilities for Muslims, contemplated religious freedom, created procedural rules regarding individuals – even created a judicial system, so disputes could be resolved.

From the standpoint of legal and State theory, fundamental rights are especially relevant to our modern age when they have been conceived as a limit to State power (its internal and external sovereignty). Consequently, the latter begins at the formation of the modern State and its evolution towards a rule of law which, on the European continent, was reaffirmed by the drive of Enlightenment thinking and constitutionalism. From this perspective, the theories of human rights and of fundamental rights[3] are

---

1 The Magna Carta was preceded by Henry I's *Charter of Liberties* of 1100.
2 On this point see, among others, the contributions of Perez (2010, 110).
3 Herein, the notion of the rights of man (from the French translation of *droits de l'homme*) and human rights (from the English translation of *human rights*) will be used interchangibly. However, the distinction between human rights and fundamental rights is more relevant: the former has a broader and, in some cases, even more imprecise meaning, while the latter have a more definite content as they are guaranteed by the (positive) legal order and, above all, by modern and contemporary constitutions where reinforced protection is foreseen. The theoretical and practical importance of this distinction still has validity, but, as will be seen

inherently linked to the processes of secularization, modern individualism and bourgeois revolutions of the seventeenth and eighteenth centuries.[4]

Human rights as a subject was raised, for the first time in modern history, albeit with a few contradictions, in teleological and legal terms, to tackle the problem of Native Americans after the conquest of America. It can be said that the *issue* of human rights was born with the first modern, global age under the sign of colonialism and genocide-ethnocide on the one hand, and the birth of international law on the other.

1.2   The universal notion of human rights through a theological and moral approach

Francisco de Vitoria, heir and devotee of Thomism,[5] theologian and graduate of the University of Salamanca, was the man who formulated, in 1539, a natural law theory in defence of Native American Indians. He is most certainly thought of as one of the most significant figures of the Spanish Renaissance (Gomez 1940, 73) and the first theoretician of international law (Scott 1939).

The Spanish thinker adopted the philosophy of Thomas Aquinas (Truyol 1946, 30) and, most of all, the Thomist proposal of a synthesis between faith and reason, which left a strong new imprint on mediaeval Christianity, by recognizing the relevance of the works of Aristotle.[6] Vitoria, like Aquinas, conceived of social life as directly subsumed within the broader system of the universe. Both men believed in a system in which human nature is *unique* among living things. Basically, humanity does not only have a material nature, but also a rational and spiritual soul which, for that very reason, makes humans more similar to God.

Like every person, native American Indians are also *similar* in the eyes of God. A human rights concept based above all on recognizing the *similar* means placing this aspect above even one's respect for the *other*, dependent

---

below, nowadays tends to be reduced by legal debates on the historical (*ergo*, fundamental) roots of human rights, by comparative law analysis on the movement of constitutional models (ergo, outside State borders) and also by studies on the protection of certain fundamental rights at the regional level (European Convention on Human Rights, European Union, etc.).

4 On this point see (Oestreich 2001, 38). In contrast, for Jellinek, the basis for the creation of a human rights culture is linked to the declaration and protection of human rights in American constitutionalism because of the struggle for religious freedom (Jellinek 1895).

5 Also in the field of post-Thomistic conceptions of Christian inspiration, the work of another Spaniar, Franciso Suárez must also be included (Milazzo 2012).

6 Various studies on the sources of the thought of Francisco de Vitoria prove a strong link with St. Thomas, St. Augustine and the scholastic theologians, as well as considerable use of Roman law and canon law texts (Barbier 1966, 46).

upon belonging to different cultures. Indeed, you could well argue that on such theological bases, the respect of the *similar* is nothing more than the recognition of each individual (and his or her unique nature) *similar* to God. In this way, the theorization of a "unique nature" prevails over cultural differences, reaffirming human dignity as, in Christianity, God himself becomes a man. That same dignity, understood and conceptualized as the dignity of the "person", even if present by its own "nature", must be recognized by a religious and/or political authority, thus making the individual a subject of the law. One need only think of the Native American Indians, who were expressed in the Papal Bull of 1537, two years before the *Relectio de Indis*, as "veri homines" because they were "fidei catholicae et sacramentum capaces".

Francisco de Vitoria's theory of human rights is, therefore, contextualized in such a way that its relevance is fully recognized. For instance, the horrific fact of slavery can be countered by stating that the Native American Indians should be treated as free people.

It's not clear, though, whether the philosopher's thoughts on human rights also extended the same dignity, not only to individuals and States in international law, but also to other cultures (including non-Christian ones). The defence of Native American Indians could well have been more of a *spiritual colonialism* presented in the form of a theological and legal conceptualization of the universality of rights.

Taking into account the right of the Spaniards to go to the Indies (the *Ius migrandi*), and at the same time, the recognition of the rights of Native American Indians, a joint reading can be made on the theological and legal attempt to balance demands of dominance (through the moderate use of violence) and to 'export' 'natural' rights to the New and barely 'discovered' World. At this stage, we can also pose another question: was this a universalism, then, which was underhandedly offering a justification to colonialism and, in certain cases, the idea of a 'just war'?[7]

Francisco de Vitoria also recognized Native American Indians rights, among others, to safety and especially to the protection of the innocent and defenceless who were still sacrificed to idols, or killed for human consumption. For these reasons, he argued that the Spaniards could not simply abandon these people in the Indies, in the midst of such a brutal regime – no, not until they had made the political and commercial changes needed to bring

---

7 The vision of universal rights from Vitoria's theological and legal point of view does not indeed oppose the idea of 'just war'. In his view, a 'purely defensive' war (the right of Spaniards to defend themselves against Indian attacks) can be legitimized, as well as a war for a 'just cause' (the right to intervene for humanitarian reasons, peace and/or security).

an end to the terror and repression[8] they were being subjected to. So, the recognition of the natural right to security and human life as well as, more generically, the recognition of all human rights, should lead to opposition of inhuman practices, in order to protect Native Americans, in some cases, not from their *fellows* (ergo, the Spaniards), but from *themselves*.

There were other motives at work behind the natural rights claim, in defence of Native Americans. In addition to the recognition of the Spaniards' right to go to the Indies. Vitoria considered legal restrictions on the colonial action of the Spanish monarchy. This was achieved through the weakening of the Crown's theocratic source[9] – the affirmation of ecclesiastical power on the "barbarians" (Native Americans) in matters related to conscience and religion. This is very interesting, because the link between these different purposes has a whole raft of implications in relation to religious freedom. The importance that Francisco de Vitoria attributed to the recognition of the natural right of nations to communicate among themselves is undeniable. This derives from the universal right to the free circulation of ideas which, in his opinion, affirmed respect for the right to spread Christ's religion across the globe (*propaganda religionis christianae*), while still respecting the rights of Native American Indians not to be baptized or forced to convert to Christianity against their will. From Vitoria's position, one which is taken up in John Locke's *A Letter Concerning Toleration* – comes the recognition, not only of the similar but also of the *other*, as the very basis of the principle of tolerance. Of course, we know full well that both the recognition and, above all, the *respect for the other* and the relevance of cultural diversity are to this day the best antidote for preventing religious wars, intolerance, racial hatred and disregard for the sanctity of human dignity.

This Salamancan theologian's approach is powerful when you look at the debates happening on the subject of tolerance across Europe from the sixteenth century and beyond, especially in the seventeenth century with the likes of Spinoza, Bayle and Locke. These were all men that shared the idea of separating political and religious powers.

The issue of religious tolerance also becomes a central theme in the American Bill of Rights, even though the adoption of the first written constitution, "a revolutionary event in the history of constitutionalism" (Matteucci 1976, 125), is rooted in the War of Independence and the demand to

8 In this case, it is lawful to make war against barbarians: "Christian princes can wage war on the barbarians, because they feed on human flesh and sacrifice men" (Vitoria 1967, 110).
9 His State theory is very significant. Although he did not use the concept of "State personality", his doctrine "contains everything that pertains to the perfect rationale behind this concept" (Naszályi 1948, 260).

establish a radically new political order to fly in the face of the European tradition,[10] valuing the federal principle above all.[11]

The conception of a 'bill of rights' also had a moral and religious root that needed to overcome some obvious contradictions: "sanctity of the privileges of race"[12] prohibited in Africa[13] and confirmed in the New World. In fact, the contradiction was evident, precisely because it had been affirmed in the Declaration of Independence of the United States of 1776, in the part in which "Jefferson includes the argument politically and philosophically harder" (Rinella 2008, 36, McIlwain 1923):

> We hold these truths to be self-evident, that all men are created equal, that they are endowed by their Creator with certain unalienable Rights, that among these are Life, Liberty and the pursuit of Happiness. – That to

10 In any case, the links between history and political, philosophical and juridical thought of the old continent are very strong, something confirmed by the influence exerted, for example, by Coke, Locke, Blackstone, Montesquieu and Rousseau. We need only think of the *common law* system, the principle of the separation of powers according to their various theories, the democratic principle and the adoption of certain legal institutions. The influence exerted by English republicanism on Machiavelli's *Discourses* is also relevant. John Adams had Machiavelli and Montesquieu as references. His works, in fact, demonstrate the importance of one of Montesquieu's central creations, *l'Esprit des Lois*, in the 1787 constitutional debate (Casalini 2005). Another link with republicanism can be found in the axis between Machiavelli and Harrington (Pocock 1975). Harrington completed his major work of 1656, *The commonwealth of Oceana*, with a very articulate and baroque draft constitution. Although the proposed institutional wording is abstract and unreal, the principle that inspires it in its entirety had notable influence on American constitutionalism: citing Aristotle (Politics, 1278b, 1282b), Harrington summarizes his opposition to Hobbes with his famous quote on the "empire of laws and not of men" (Matteucci 1992). Similarly, Pettit and Skinner agree with Pocock regarding Machiavelli's recovery of the Roman tradition, Harrington's revision, and the incorporation of American revolutionaries (Pettit 1997; Skinner 1998). Finally, the influence of English republicanism is confirmed by the most meticulous comparative evolutionary studies on some legal institutions, such as the presidential veto, with precise reference to the English *Instrument of Government* of 1653 (Buratti 2012, 31).
11 It is interesting to note that the fundamental concepts of Federal theology are present in Cauvin's thinking, as well as the works of Scottish theologian, Robert Rollock.
12 According to Engels (1974, 101), because of the eminently bourgeois nature of human rights "it is significant of the specifically bourgeois character of these human rights that the American constitution, the first to recognise the rights of man, in the same breath confirms the slavery of the coloured races existing in America: class privileges are proscribed, race privileges sanctified".
13 In the various human rights stories, it is often forgotten that the African Mandé Charter was adopted in 1222, on the day of the coronation of Sundiata Keïta as emperor of Mali, and that it prohibited slavery, for it was considered the origin of every conflict, and also contained provisions on the protection of life, liberty, solidarity, justice and equality.

secure these rights, Governments are instituted among Men, deriving their just powers from the consent of the governed, – That whenever any Form of Government becomes destructive of these ends, it is the Right of the People to alter or to abolish it, and to institute new Government, laying its foundation on such principles and organizing its powers in such form, as to them shall seem most likely to affect their Safety and Happiness.

It is this idea, of one's inalienable rights, which also explains why, as we will see later,[14] Edmund Burke was so vocal in favour of the American revolution and on the other hand, so extremely critical of the French revolution. Indeed, there is no denying the moral and religious matrix of natural law present in the American Bill of Rights. It even states that "the individual, not thanks to the State, but by its very nature is endowed with juridical subjectivity" and that, therefore, "possesses inalienable and intangible rights" (Jellinek 1895). This is the first synthesis of relevance, on a historical level, between universal instances and positive demands: for the very first time, American constitutionalism is linked to natural and universal constitutionalism. The fundamental principles of natural law were positivized, becoming part of the written constitution of the United States. It might be more correct to say that its formalization was almost immediate: it is enough to think that the first 10 amendments were adopted in 1791, though they were applied gradually. Other parts of natural law and 'innate' natural rights lost some of their immediate validity, until the State evolved and established them as constitutive and fundamental principles.

In American constitutional history, the 'innate' rights established in the Declaration of Independence, which echo the ideas of the English levellers, are 'conquered' by the settlers in the War of Independence and 'snatched' from the 'savages': legislators cite conflicts of indigenous populations, with their burden of atrocity, as an example. On the other hand, in the US Constitution and the Bill of Rights there is no reference to natives' rights.[15] In addition, through the Indian Commerce Clause, which attributes the exclusive competence to trade with indigenous communities to federal (and not state) authorities, the US federal government progressively made its own powers over native populations felt – beyond issues of trade.

---

14 See Section 1.4 of this chapter.
15 However, as is well known, in Canada, the Constitution Act of 1982 provides for the introduction of the rights of indigenous peoples in the constitutional charter. The guarantee granted to Aboriginal rights in the constitution has been strengthened through various amendment procedures. In fact, in 1983, it was established that every amendment of constitutional provisions related to rights of indigenous peoples should be done by arranging a constitutional conference.

Consequently, the theological and moral foundations of the theory of innate rights were hit by demands of domination and control of the new territories and demands by the Southern states (concerning slavery), whose economy was bound up in agriculture. A few decades after the Declaration of Independence, as well as during the Civil War of 1861–1865, there were already moral reasons to combat slavery, along with reasons connected to the conflict between the differing economies of the agricultural Southern states and the (industrialized)[16] Northern states.

1.3 The rational conception of "natural rights" based on an empirical perspective

Today, there is still a distinction made in the United Kingdom and the United States between 'moral rights' and 'legal rights' – something similar to that made in European courts of law, between natural and positive rights. In both cases, this is a distinction between two normative systems that, for Anglo-Saxon jurists, does not bring about any separation. In fact, in the common law system, natural rights are – by tradition – the rights of 'Englishmen' – meaning that the link with the *lex terrae*, or the 'law of the land', can never be forgotten.

According to Coke (who with Selden was one of the main architects of the Petition of Right),[17] the common law system could only be understood as a matter of blind faith in tradition, representing an artificial perfection of reason. It was not understood as a natural reason or an innate intelligence, common to all people; the "artificial reason" which he talked about was describing lawyers who understood the law as an agreement. They were not taking into account doctrines and laws, as much as observation and experience as elements that characterized the legal profession. This explains why Coke, in a key decision of 1607 (*Case of Prohibitions del Roy*), openly questioned James I's claim to be a "judge" in one of his own courts,[18]

---

16 Since the second half of the nineteenth century, the industrial revolution, which had already reached England, Belgium, part of France and certain parts of Germany, arrived not only in other European countries, as it did in Italy, but also crossed the pond, making its presence felt even in the United States.

17 One cannot share Sabine's (1981, 346) thesis, according to which Coke was "an absolute conservative and more of a reactionary" (Bonfiglio 2009, 20).

18 "The King in his own person cannot adjudge any case, either criminal or betwixt party and party; but it ought to be determined and adjudged in some Court of Justice, according to the law and custom of England" (Prohibitions, Case of [1607] EWHC KB J23, 01 November 1607). In order to analyze the issue in depth, see Conklin (1979), Sacco (1991), Moccia (2001), and Mattei (2014).

arguing that natural reason alone was simply not enough to provide justice – he would also need to be technically prepared.[19]

Coke came up with the concept of artificial reason by looking at the judge as an instrument of cultural and institutional integration – a role now confirmed by a "creative" jurisprudence (in other words, the interpretative and paralegislative judgements of constitutional courts).

Another absolutely crucial decision Coke made, this time in 1610 (sitting as Chief Justice of the Common Pleas) was *Bonham's Case*. Here, he established the power of common law judges to control and annul acts, even if they came from Parliament, that went against justice, reason, or even if they were reprehensible or unenforceable. Thus, said Coke, the common law system existed independent of and superior to statutes. In that ruling, Coke assessed the role of the judge as interpreter and guarantor of the supremacy of constitutional principles and rules. In fact, when the supremacy of Parliament was confirmed after the 'Glorious Revolution', the superiority of the rule of law that limited the sovereign through a non-State law, in other words, the common law, was not lost on anyone.

Coke's artificial reason has nothing to do with 'faith' in reason or with abstract logicism (the philosophy of mathematics that believes most things can be reduced to logic), but in a certain sense, pre-empts Grozio's rational method: the evocation of reason which does not exclude the observation of empirical facts.

It is thanks to Dutch jurist and philosopher Hugo Grozio that we now have an accurate definition of *ius*, as an inherent quality of the person. From this subjectivization of the law, manifested in the first pages of his main work of 1625 *De iure belli ac pacis*, human rights are born, but not from a theological and religious point of view, as in the case of Francisco de Vitoria. Grozio, though profoundly Christian and a promoter of religious unity,

---

19 Prohibitions, Case of [1607] EWHC KB J23, 01 November 1607: "A controversy of land between parties was heard by the King, and sentence given, which was repealed for this, that it did not belong to the common law: then the King said, that he thought the law was founded upon reason, and that he and others had reason, as well as the Judges: to which it was answered by me, that true it was, that God had endowed His Majesty with excellent science, and great endowments of nature; but His Majesty was not learned in the laws of his realm of England, and causes which concern the life, or inheritance, or goods, or fortunes of his subjects, are not to be decided by natural reason but by the *artificial reason and judgement of law, which law is an act which requires long study and experience*, before that a man can attain to the cognizance of it: that the law was the golden met-wand and measure to try the causes of the subjects; and which protected His Majesty in safety and peace: with which the King was greatly offended, and said, that then he should be under the law, which was treason to affirm, as he said; to which I said, that Bracton saith, [That the King ought not to be under any man but under God and the law.]" (emphasis added).

was also a strong supporter of the separation between Church and State. In other words, for Grozio, natural law did not need justification in the will of God or in the divine order of things, because it is independent from God's existence: natural order is a result of human rationality.

Beginning with Grozio, the observation of empirical facts also appears in the modern theory of natural rights, based on a political contract, even in its different versions (such as Selden and Hobbes, for example).[20] The contract is established on 'rational' grounds, in accordance with the English tradition of the 'contract', stipulated by the king and barons in the Magna Carta, the pact par excellence. So, just as the contract creates rights and obligations, the political contract establishes a covenant between social parties.

In the contractual conception of Thomas Hobbes, consensus provides the emergence of the State, to which there is utmost obedience. The contract, which entails the alienation of all natural rights but one (the right to life), requires a pledge of absolute obedience to the sovereign, who, in turn, guarantees the individual life security, as its supreme legal interest. The definition of civil law in *Leviathan,*[21] his main work, responds to the principle *auctoritas non veritas facit legem*. Therefore, his contractual conception presents elements that on the one hand entail a clear break with respect to the theory of natural rights, but on the other precede the theory of legal positivism.

Locke's contractualism, in contrast to Hobbes, reveals more elements of continuity with Althusius's and Grozio's natural law theory, and even with the work of Richard Hooker, who Locke was thought to be a disciple of.

Like Marsilio de Padua,[22] Hooker[23] emphasized popular consensus as the only valid foundation of a political society. More specifically, unlike Hobbes, according to Hooker a verifiable consensus is not only useful for the genesis of a state, but also after its institutional building.

---

20 Take Selden and Hobbes as examples, regardless of their political differences, for both initiated a modern theory of natural rights (Tuck 1981). While Hobbes argued that the sovereign was conceived as a non-contracting third party, Selden thought that the monarch was part of the contract. Concerning Locke's notion of contract, it seems to be closer to the approach of continental writers, such as Althusius and Pufendorf, who "put forth two contracts, one between individuals from which the community arises, and another between the community and its government. Locke tacitly assumes a similar stance, though he never defended explicitly" (Sabine 1981, 408).
21 This is his most famous and important work on political philosophy, published in 1651. See the edition with Italian, English and Latin texts coord. by Raffaella Santi, 2001.
22 His main work is *Defensor pacis* of 1324.
23 *Laws of ecclesial polity* was his main work, divided into eight books, the first of which were published in 1595, the fifth in 1697 and the remaining three after his death (between 1648 and 1662) (see http://anglicanhistory.org/hooker/).

While Hooker, like Alusio, proposes a State theory which stresses the notion of *populus*,[24] Locke – whose influence in explaining "the glorious fortune of natural law" (Bobbio 1963, 4) should not be underestimated – makes it more relevant via the contractual conception between individuals, given it attaches greater importance as an original contract, with respect to the creation of a given government. But he does not look at its ordinary aspect as irrelevant for liberty's sake. Consequently, it is necessary to affirm the constitutional principle of separation of powers, so that the executive and the legislative power do not fall into the same hands. This is an idea that, though it has taken a general theoretical form, is strongly linked to English constitutional history and, for this very reason, is different to that which, much later down the line, Montesquieu formulated.

In his theory, at the beginning of the separation of powers, Locke adds the principle of coordination and the principle of balance between political forces (corresponding to the Aristotelian distinction). The federal function, conceived as an autonomous function which allows for action in the sphere of international relations and the executive function, is attributed to the King. Conversely, the legislative function is attributed to the Crown and the Assemblies. For Locke, there is no reference to the jurisdictional function, which can be easily explained by the nature of the common law system, as shared customary rules developed by judges, or by the fact that the highest peak of the judicial hierarchy was the House of Lords, whose mission was to enact customary rules, as a last resort. It is well known that this very close, organic relationship between jurisdictional and legislative functions in the case of England was upset only in 2005, by the Constitutional Reform Act and the establishment of the Supreme Court of the United Kingdom, which has since 1 October 2009 assumed the Law Lords' jurisdictional function.

The real issue with Locke's philosophical thought is in the seeming imbalance between his empiricism towards the theory of knowledge and his theory on the right to private property, understood as a typical right in rem, being the remaining natural rights of a similar nature. Indeed, his writings defending religious freedom would be more coherent with the whole of his philosophical thought in their historical context, given that, in eighteenth-century England, it could have been almost a reality (mostly because, as the Test Act was still in force, Catholics and dissidents were still deprived of civil rights).

---

24 Hence, *pactum societatis* and *pactum subiectiones* adopted a constitutional meaning as fundamental principles of the state organization apparatus, though never implying full individual autonomy (Galizia 1951, 178).

In his famous work, *A Letter Concerning Toleration*,[25] Locke argues that:

> The toleration of those that differ from others in matters of religion is so agreeable to the Gospel of Jesus Christ, and to the genuine reason of mankind, that it seems monstrous for men to be so blind as not to perceive the necessity and advantage of it in so clear a light.
>
> (Locke 1689b)

In this book, Erasmian roots undermine his alleged individualism, which, from a historical point of view, is an invention of which Locke's critics and later policy theorists have taken advantage.[26] So, the interpretation of Locke's writings on tolerance as an individualistic theory is not correct, unless the reader wants to strip his writings of their actual content, including "the assumption that Christianity possesses a charitable character and that there is a minimum ethical understanding found in any given society" (Viano 2005, 29).

If Locke's presumed individualism is, in fact, weakened in his work on tolerance, his psychological explanation, on the contrary, stays fully anchored in his empiricism. He maintains that a distinction has to be made between the interest of civil society and religion, and that there must be distinct boundaries established between Church and State: "If each of them would stay within its own bounds – one attending to the worldly welfare of the commonwealth, the other to the salvation of souls – there couldn't possibly be any discord between them" (Locke 1689b). Locke demonstrates that the care of souls cannot come under the jurisdiction of the civil magistrates, which should be limited to the care and protection of public interests – such as life, liberty, freedom from bodily illness and pain, and the possession of worldly things. The Church can only be a *free and voluntary society*, always giving those who wish to leave it the opportunity to do so, with the same freedom with which they entered:

> And anyway the life and power of true religion consists in faith, faith involves believing·, and no-one can just believe what someone else tells him to believe, even if he wants to. [. . .] It can't be up to the magistrate to take care of souls, because his power consists only in outward force, whereas true and saving religion consists in the inward faith of the soul.
>
> (Locke 1689b)

25 Published in Latin in 1689 and drafted during his exile in Holland, Locke, in *A Letter Concerning Toleration*, dropped 'sociological' considerations that appeared in his previous 1677 *Essay concerning Toleration*.
26 See Viano (2005, 28).

Reading this quotation, Locke's psychological stance couldn't be any clearer.

Let us return to the relationship between Locke's empirical theory of knowledge and his theory of property. Locke's defence of property as a typical "natural" right in rem adopts a rational approach that includes empirical observation. Unsurprisingly, the landowning wealthy class were wildly opposed to Locke's individual rights doctrine and, in particular, his theory which proposed property as the outcome of human labour. An individual's property, he explained, also included work carried out by one's own hands. Locke writes: "Whatsoever then he removes out of the state that nature hath provided, and left it in, he hath mixed his labour with, and joined to it something that is his own, and thereby makes it his property" (Locke 1690, 249).

What does this mean? It means the right to private property is created as a natural and simultaneously empirical right. Its historical development and explanation are psychological and so, attributable to his empirical theory of knowledge.

Despite its shortfalls, it is with good reason that the leading representatives of the eighteenth-century Scottish Enlightenment revisited the empirical paradigms of the Lockean philosophical matrix, in the light of Newton's teachings – particularly by Hume through strong criticism of *iusnaturalism* in his *Treatise of Human Nature*, published between 1739 and 1740. The most fascinating epistemological aspects of the Scottish Enlightenment are in fact connected to the reception of the analytic-inductive method, a method applicable to all kinds of research – whatever the field or sector. It involves the rejection of abstract principles, but not general ones, via transition from the particular to the universal.

If all the main commercial writers were English, it is no small coincidence that their biggest critics were exponents of the Scottish Enlightenment. In fact, Hume's and Smith's critique of commercialism was a critique of the State discipline of economic life, and it supported free competition through the use of 'trade'[27] against protectionism, which had proved useful in consolidating State power and strengthening centralized pressures.

1.4 The socio-historical conception of rights and freedoms in contrast to "universal rights"

A true historical notion of the law and rights is one that arises from experience and English legal culture. It is impossible to detach rights from their

27 'Trade' is understood in a broad sense, comprising all the dynamic aspects of economic life: from the relationships between individuals to legal institutions that regulate legal activities linked to trade.

historical links. The Magna Carta, the Petition of Rights, and other documents associated with constitutional sources of law, confirm a method and notion that we could define as a constant adaptation of rights:[28] not to revolutionize them but to adapt them to an existing reality, accommodating both individuals and their socio-historical context.

As stated before, both in Coke's artificial reason and Locke's conception of natural law, there is no clash between reason and custom. When looking at English 'revolutions', there are elements of greater environmental continuity and partial institutional discontinuity. The latter can best be explained by comparing it with the successive French revolutionary experience and its different approach to rights, with respect to its English counterpart. Beyond the English Channel, 'natural rights' are the 'rights of the English'. Look at the France case, and human rights are considerably more abstract, detached from concrete use and praxis, for political, economic and social reasons that require an obvious 'breakdown' of the *ancien régime*. It was this which gave birth to a kind of faith in the omnipotence of the Enlightenment (Holbach) and progress (Turgot and Condorcet) in France in the eighteenth century. Surely it is no mere coincidence that the most important French political writers are far removed from the prevailing currents of the French Enlightenment: Montesquieu, on the one hand, and Rousseau on the other?

Montesquieu's *De l'esprit des lois* (1748),[29] does not extract principles from prejudice, but from the "nature of things", as reflected by its author in the *Prefacio*, and uses the principles themselves with special reference to the various forms of State and government. In studying the "nature of things", Montesquieu pays close attention to environmental factors, relativism of political values, their impact on institutions and the relationships between all these elements, as factors which shape the "spirit of laws". In this context, moderate government and freedom are the result of public morality and good State organization. Montesquieu, greatly influenced by the English constitutional experience, seeks a structure of power that can revive the old French freedoms. But their concept of separation of powers is not entirely legal, given that powers are returned to the social elements

---

28 On this point see, among others, the contributions of Torre (2007).

29 Montesquieu's masterpiece was well received in eighteenth-century Italy, exercising a great and complex influence, particularly on Cesare Beccaria, Antonio Genovesi, Gaetano Filangieri, Pietro Verri, Dalmazzo Francesco Vasco and Vittorio Alfieri. This influence extends well into the nineteenth century, reaching, for example, Vincenzo Cuoco, Gian Domenico Romagnosi, Antonio Rosmini and, above all, Federico Scoppis di Salerano, author of two relevant works concerning Montesquieu. After World War II, the first monographs on the French thinker belong to Vidal (1950) and Cotta (1953). Among the numerous subsequent works, see Felice (1998). Also noteworthy is the excellent collection of the works of the French thinker Felice (2014), with the French text attached.

that characterize them; so following the 'spirit of the laws', Montesquieu entrusts the attributions of the different State functions to certain social entities, in order to maintain a system of checks and balances. He believes the legislative power should be conferred to a body of nobles and a body of representatives of the people, while the executive power should remain in the hands of the monarch. However, unlike the theories on government that appeared in ancient times (Polybius), this French thinker emphasizes a theory of modern government focused not so much the horizontal separation – between the different classes – of power but the attributions of the main functions of the State for each organ, which needed to be independent from each other.[30]

It is crucial to highlight, however, that both the traditional theory of mixed government and Montesquieu's writings on moderate government do not conform to Rousseau's approach. Rousseau's influential work, although particular and complex, even inspired the Declaration of the Rights of Man and of the Citizen, approved by the National Assembly on 29 August 1789. For example, this statement contains a reference to the "general will" as the holder of legislative power (Article 6), a reference that is not found in the American Declaration of Independence.

The Geneva-born philosopher is not an illuminist, but rather an advocate of natural or universal rights. In his view, there are no "natural" rights and, so, even the right to private property is not a natural but a collective right, recognized as such. For Locke, as already stated, property rights are rights that belong to the individual in an obvious way, while Rousseau (1765), in his *Constitutional Project for Corsica*, provides that "property of the state to be as large and strong, that of the citizens as small and weak, as possible". In his eyes, human rights do not exist, only those rights and duties of the citizen; there is no morality outside of society, and it is not the person, but the citizen who becomes the fundamental moral category.

Both the rediscovery of 'community' and the consideration of the equality principle are the distinctive lines of Rousseau's political philosophy. In some cases, however, there is a certain prevalence of an idea of community closer to that of city-state, as well as of a citizenship founded and nourished exclusively on national sentiment. This is the case, for example, with his appeal to Polish nationalism in his work on Poland (Rousseau 1772a). Given his concept of community as an organic whole, not a group of individuals, the Swiss philosopher appears as the theoretician of a freedom not fit for the modern world (Constant 1819),[31] as was emphasized by Constant,

---

30 The separation of powers, as a formula to not accumulate normative, executive and control functions "is, more than ever, current events" (Silvestri 1984, 250; Modugno 1966, 477).
31 For a deeper study of Constant's work, see, in Italy, De Luca (1993, 2003).

whose political and constitutional basis[32] is grounded upon solid empirical liberalism (Barberis 1984, 1988). The same principles, according to Constant, have an empirical basis because they are constructed from events, circumstances and cultural debate, and are, therefore, the result of a complex socio-historical interaction.

According to Rousseau, mixed government in a republican form of State also has a democratic basis, even though a purely democratic government, both in form and in governance, is better adapted to a city than to an entire nation.[33] The democratic basis for this is the principle of equality. In his *Constitutional Project for Corsica*, using the experience of the Swiss Protestant cantons as his model, Rousseau (1765) argues that the fundamental principle of the constitution for Corsica must be equality: "Everything must be related to it, including even authority, which is established only to defend it. All should be equal by right of birth".

Unlike Rousseau, "the main reason for Burke's aversion to a human rights theory is to be found in anti-egalitarianism" (Martinelli 2014, 56) and in his firm aversion to the Jacobin theory of popular sovereignty.[34] Burke is not a reactionary like Maistre; perhaps qualifying him as a liberal reformist is more suitable.[35] He emanates a sort of worship for tradition that leads him to an Anglo-centric idealization of history, which, nonetheless, contradicts his recognized realistic approach. Burke is a convinced conservative: in his resolute attack on abstract principles of French revolutionary radicalism,[36] he points to "natural rights" and not to "natural law", taking a classical or scholastic approach.

Can there be anything more abstract than 'innate' rights claimed by American settlers? Burke's position was not contrary, but rather in support of the settlers, since the religious and moral concept inferred by 'innate' rights

---

32 According to Bastid (1966, 923), in Constant's constitutional theory, the separation between royal and ministerial powers was no more than the axis of liberal monarchy. Constant notes that "the mere fact that the monarch is inviolable and that the ministers are responsible proves that separation" (Cerroni 1979, 63).

33 In the Constitutional Project for Corsica, Rousseau (1765) states that "it would be impossible to bring together the whole people of an island like those of a city; and when the supreme authority is entrusted to delegates, the government changes and becomes aristocratic. What Corsica needs is a mixed government, where the people assemble by Articles rather than as a whole, and where the repositories of its power are changed at frequent intervals".

34 For more on the difference between natural law and revolutionary 'natural rights', see Stanlis (2009, 245), who points out, "Burke believed not in the Jacobin or Rousseauist heresy of *vox populi, vox Dei*, but in a civil order founded upon constitutional law and Natural Law".

35 As for the counterrevolutionary Catholic thought of De Maistre or Bonald, Burke was not a 'reformist', but solely a 'liberal' thinker.

36 His essay on the French revolution of 1790 has been very influential.

stems from the ancient freedoms of the English, which were the root of their historical rights. The French, however, had lost their old freedoms. For this reason, Montesquieu naturally casts his critical eye beyond the English Channel when thinking of France, and a moderate government which could guarantee political freedom.

Before 1789, the situation in France was dramatically different to that of the England of 1688. French political radicalism was the result of an economic, political, social and moral crisis that had led to a 'true' bourgeois social revolution against the *ancien régime*, a revolution that would have decimated neither centralism nor the absolute conception of sovereignty. However, the 'glorious' English revolution (which was not exactly traumatic), if anything held onto a clear continuity with English constitutional tradition.

In France, the consequences of these revolutionary events were very soon characterized by their evolution from abstract universalism of human rights into interference, annexation, wars of conquest,[37] or 'passive' revolution, as was seen during the Neapolitan revolution of 1799 (Cuoco 1801),[38] as well as during the empire of Napoleon I and Napoleon III, who ordered General Oudinot to help Pius IX and overthrow the Roman Republic (Desmos 2012, 129).

1.5 The conception of freedom-based rights: from its declaration to its first constitutional embodiment

The first stage of 1789 is linked to the general proclamation of universal rights – in its political and, to a certain extent, ideological version[39] – described by Tocqueville (1856) as a time of "generous and sincere passions". In contrast, both the revolutionary and post-revolutionary work, which had significant repercussions on the European continent, are united by the expectation of incorporating the Declaration into the preambles of the 1791, 1793 and 1795 constitutions, but in a new, extended version.[40]

---

37 Until the decree of 22 May 1790, revolutionary France had renounced any war based on conquest and undertook not to apply its force against the liberty of any community (Boudon 2012, 97).
38 He was influenced by Giambattista Vico, and therefore rejected the rational component of the Enlightenment due to its broad, abstract nature. For a detailed analysis of the relationship between the concept of 'passive revolution' and the Italian Risorgimento, see Gramsci's (1975) essays.
39 "Only in the name of the general [universal] rights of society can a particular class vindicate for itself general domination" (Marx 1844a). See, in particular, his criticism of the French Declaration (Marx 1843).
40 In the 1793 constitution, the 17 original provisions became 35. In the 1795 Constitution, there were 22 provisions on rights and 9 related to obligations. The constitution of 1799, on

Those implications were significant, even in the United Kingdom. Burke's attack on the French revolution was a political and ideological response to Fox's stance in favour of the 1789 revolution. Burke reiterated his fear that the revolutionary movement could spread in England and, for this reason, as Thomas Paine reproached him in his famous book *Rights of Man*, its main adversaries were not so much the French revolutionary theorists, but Burke's English henchmen.

Likewise, post-revolutionary work is supported by the fact that the 1789 Declaration concluded a subjective process of natural law theory, so that a constant, and essentially bipolar, dialectic between authority and freedom emerged. After the French revolution, policies that favoured the universal recognition of rights prevailed in the nineteenth century. This was balanced out by the effective primacy of the executive branch over the legislative branch, despite favourable theorization towards the latter, which imposed some limits on the exercise of fundamental freedoms.

Analysis of the constitutions of the Napoleonic period confirms that rights related to liberty were not included, with the exception of the Additional Act to the Constitutions of the Empire (also known as the Charter of 1815), which the liberal Constant[41] helped to draft. In addition, the Napoleonic Criminal Code of 1810 established an extension of death penalty cases, a hardening of criminal theory against the State and a general increase in the scope of criminal sanctions.

Not surprisingly, the aforementioned trend coincides with the emergence of the concept of public order and its inclusion, for the first time, in the Napoleonic Code – the true constitution of the then-triumphant bourgeois class. The concept was mentioned, but not defined, acquiring a rather vague nature. This is arguably still the case today, as it is often attributed a multiplicity of meanings, including the notion of (public) security and its 'protective' function against 'internal enemies' and, against 'external enemies' in the case of other legal systems. Public order was directed, in this case,

---

the other hand, omits its incorporation and the Napoleonic of 1804 contained no reference to the human rights.

41 Constant is considered the father of liberal nineteenth-century constitutionalism. However, for a long time in Italy, he was mistakenly considered a 'minor' thinker in comparison to Montesquieu and Tocqueville, and some of his works took longer to translate. Not many scholars, for example, are aware that Constant has two different works with the same title: *Principles of Politics Applicable to All Governments*. The 1815 essay is a kind of commentary on the new constitution, while the 1806 draft is presented as a true systematic discourse, which was completed by Constant while in 'exile' in Switzerland and is distinctly anti-Napoleonic in nature. Everything he published from 1814 to 1830 can be "extracted" from the 1806 version, including his famous 1819 discourse on the *Liberty of the Ancients Compared with that of the Moderns*.

towards the restoration and defence of the legal order and property, as a supreme value.

Within Europe, public order and its limiting function to rights and freedoms, through a State-centric approach, reaffirmed that the recognition of a right to liberty vis-à-vis the State, derived from 'self-limitation' of the State itself. It drew partly on the strictly positivist view whereby state self-limitation was to be understood as the basis of the rights to liberty.

However, the era of the Restoration did not constitute a return to the *ancien régime*: during the nineteenth century various constitutional texts were adopted confirming liberty rights and the formation of liberal States in the face of revolutionary democratic radicalism. The origin of the doctrine of national sovereignty, according to Bacot (1985, 125), does not lie in the French revolution, but came into being during the revolution, in order to distinguish popular sovereignty from national sovereignty.

In asserting national sovereignty, the bourgeois social hegemony was consolidated. The bourgeoisie found their most significant expression in the political institutions of the Orleanist monarchy, after the 1814 charter and the attempt of Carlos X to transform the absolutist constitutional monarchy, restricting freedom of the press and electoral laws, with no legislative basis. These acts caused the Paris riots, bringing about the Orleanist monarchy and the 1830 charter, the latter being more advanced with respect to its predecessor. The 1830 charter sought to re-establish the balance between powers and abolished the principle of State religion and censorship, while updating electoral laws. A few years later, in 1834,[42] the first Constitutional Law Chair was created in France,[43] its purpose to explain the political institutions established under the 1830 monarchical charter. This clearly shows the political origin of French constitutionalist doctrine, stemming from the consolidation of the monarchical principle affirmed both in the 1814 (Madame de Staël 1818)[44] and 1830 charters.

Between 1830 and 1848, there was a rapid development of constitutionalism, whose clearest expression on the European continent was to be found in the Belgian Constitution of 1831, beginning with the recognition and conferral of certain rights. In this regard, Dicey writes:

---

42 Before that date, at the end of the eighteenth century, the faculty chairs for the teaching of this subject were awarded to Compagnoni, Alpruni and Algerati from the three universities of the Cisalpine Republic: Ferrara, Pavia and Bologna, respectively. Morelli (1898, 63–111) has the merit of correcting the belief that the chair of Paris was *prior in tempore*.

43 The aforementioned chair was Rossi (1866).

44 Staël-Holstein was known by the alias Madame de Staël; her posthumous work was published in 1818. A new edition can be found in Volume II, Charpentier, Libraire-Éditeur, Paris, 1862, pages 248, 414 and 450.

The Belgian constitution indeed comes very near to a written repro-
duction of the English constitution, and the constitution of England
might easily be turned into an Act of Parliament without suffering any
material transformation of character, provided only that the English
Parliament retained – what the Belgian Parliament, by the way, does
not possess – the unrestricted power of repealing or amending the constitutional code.

(Dicey 1885, 38–39)

The Belgian Constitution of 1831, in fact, already foresaw a special constitutional revision procedure.[45]

After the 1830 and 1831 revolts,[46] the consolidation of the bourgeois
order coincided with the transition from Enlightenment to Positivism. Both
cases involved two philosophical and cultural currents of bourgeois roots,
with diverse yet sound bases in France and England: the first, radically critical and revolutionary; the second, viable with respect to the constituted
order. Auguste Comte identified himself politically as a conservative and,
at the same time, as a progressive in a scientific sense. Nineteenth-century
positivism became a kind of conservative Enlightenment, from an ideological perspective.

It is not so surprising then that, as Mortati writes, "the elasticity of constitutional rules in the pseudo-liberal constitutions of the nineteenth century allowed to try and reserve the maximum power to the ultimate state

45 According to Article 131 of the Belgian Constitution of 1831: "The federal legislative
power has the right to declare that there are reasons to revise such constitutional provision
as it determines. Following such a declaration, the two Houses are automatically dissolved.
Two new Chambers will be convened, in accordance with the provisions of Article 71.
These Houses make decisions, in common accord with the King, on the points submitted
for revision. In this case, the Houses can only debate provided that at least two thirds of
the members who make up each House are present; and no change is adopted unless it is
supported by at least two thirds of the votes cast".

46 After the harsh repression of the revolts of 1820–1821, the rebellions of 1830–1831, especially in Spain – whose epicentre was not, in fact, Paris – brought the Orlean 'bourgeois
monarchy' to France. After the 1848 revolts, in contrast, conservative modernization with
a liberal approach took place throughout Europe. Take the Albertine Statute of 1848, as
one of the many liberal constitutions adopted by sovereigns, as an example. In France,
discouragement of the most disadvantaged classes led to the 1848 revolution, which would
end in the bloody annihilation of the 'Paris Commune'. After repressive army intervention,
the French constitution of 1848 was adopted, representative of the high bourgeoisie and
industrial class, but also as an expression of the middle class. The republican experience,
however, had a very short duration due to the coup d'état of 2 December 1851 and the new
constitution, which came into force in 1852 and which consecrated the authoritarian power
of Louis Napoleon, making him emperor under the name of Napoleon III.

authority to repress freedoms, so recognized in a generic form" (Mortati 1986, 181).

In contrast to the United Kingdom, during the second half of the nineteenth century, Germany's modernization had a clear conservative cut. In France, after the liberal experience of the Orleanist 'bourgeois monarchy', the fall of Napoleon III's empire, the birth of the 1875 'conservative republic' and the bloody and grave repression of the second Paris 'Commune' more representative and liberal institutions were created. This was also the case in Italy, during the statutory period, before the advent of Fascism.

1.6 The conception of freedom-based rights: between nationalism and rigid legal positivism

From the second half of the nineteenth century onwards, idealism was replaced by naturalism, as Darwin's Theory of Evolution was quickly embraced in Germany (Pinkard 2014, 430). Similarly, in a post-Hegelian nineteenth century, more conservative currents and forces prevailed.

The Hegelian right was hostile to change and brought a conservative emphasis to the interpretation of the established order: *what is real is rational.* This position was useful when counteracting the revolutionary Hegelian left, which, alternately, highlighted criticism and a need for change: *what is rational is real.*

This demonstrates how closely method is linked to the political and philosophical views that lie behind it (Wilhelm 1958). Anti-Hegelian positivists praise the concretion of scientific knowledge and of 'what is put or placed' (from Latin *positum*), that is, reality. However, even an understanding of the facts may depend on how they are consciously ordered in our thinking. Heller writes:

> It does not exist [. . .] a fact in its pure state, given that any understanding of facts requires it to be systematic. Metaphysics is always inevitable, even for legal positivism. Each positivist has their own metaphysical ontology and ethics that are distinguished from conscious meta-physician solely by their naivety and insufficient control over metaphysics.
>
> (Heller 1929, 366)

Considered as it may have been "fruit of a colossal deception" (Heller 1929, 365), positivism in State and Legal Theory prevailed in the second half of the nineteenth century – encouraging the use of theory as a technique to describe the existing power apparatus. In addition, positivism also considered the problem of principles in legal science[47] and individual rights in relation to the State on a secondary level. So, prevailing over legal formalism, a somewhat hostile tendency towards citizens' rights with regards to the State emerged, denying or admitting rights with reservations and limitations, and practically nullifying the value of their general reception.

For example, Laband consciously blends formalistic and political tendencies in his theoretical approach, thus consolidating himself as "true and authentic lawyer of the crown" (Nigro 1973, 296). The German lawyer's distinction between formal and material rules are closely linked to his political objectives, given his desire to consolidate power in the monarchy. That said, Gerber's work – inspired by the search for greater stringency, which led him to give more relevance to positive data – is not the fruit of a wholly formalist approach. In his work *Über öffentliche Rechte* (1852) there is an overlap between the State and the monarch and, in his subsequent works *Grundzüge des deutschen Staatssrechts* (1865), we can observe a liberal view of the State.

Gerber sought to refine scientific dogma on positive Public Law, through a Private Law approach. This search, which led to *Grundzüge* (1865), served to build a *system* inspired by a unitary idea that would conquer German Public Law's own autonomy.

At the same time, in Italy, Vittorio Emanuele Orlando developed his 'twist' approach during his 1885, 1886 and 1889 academic activity in Modena, Messina and Palermo, respectively.

Orlando's 'scientific revolution', in pursuit of a domestic law, was also encouraged by greater rigour with respect to theory and strong patriotism.[48] The distinction between legal and political order, as defended by the Sicilian jurist in terms of a more rigorous method, had a clear political function: it was not enough to sustain State unity; it had to be reinforced and become a reality through domestic Public Law. According to Orlando, it was vital to "consider different concepts and legal institutions as real, existing and living entities" (Orlando 1889, 9). In my view, it is a question of hypothesizing

---

47 However, most of nineteenth-century German doctrine tended to reject natural law theories, which were still influential. For instance, Savigny (1814) used the principles (*Grudsätze*), not only as a heuristic instrument, but also to individualize research principles and to reach the material roots of legal science research.

48 In spite of being paradoxical, the importance of Orlando's idea lies "in the political function of the legal method" (Cassese 2011, 310). Orlando, according to Sabino Cassese, "feels like the heir of the patriots and statists of the Risorgimento; suffered the constitutional shortcomings of the new State" (Cassese 2011, 310). For this reason, the main purpose of Orlando's reflection was the consolidation of a new State, through the affirmation of a "new science" (Azzariti 2011, 123).

about concepts and institutions with the support of a systematic sensitivity or a conscious choice of adherence to the existing State: hence Orlando's science-based argument, divergent from that of Gerber and Laband, on the Italian form of government that conciliates *Rechsstaat* and the notion of parliamentary government (Orlando 1886, 521–586).

Orlando's more liberal positioning with respect to the two aforementioned German jurists is also confirmed by his interest in Jellinek's work on the theory of "subjective public rights". Orlando's extensive Public Law studies cannot hide his bias towards the major philosophical school of thought and method manifest in the works of Jellinek (Orlando 1912) on subjective public rights. This theory was further outlined in *Allgemeine Staatslehre*.[49] However, Orlando adds that Jellinek's greatest merit is to have detached himself from the leading view in Germany, by not only recognizing the existence of subjective public rights, but also by assigning them "an extension and, most importantly, a function that can qualify as essential and vital, in the field of Public Law" (Orlando 1912, 278). According to Orlando, it is thanks to Jellinek that the focus on German legal science in favour of citizens' rights with regards to the State acquires "a particular value for it constitutes a fundamental *trait d'union* between Latin and German-speaking political and scientific trends" (Orlando 1912, 279).

By contrast, in Italy, a rather restrictive interpretation of the State's self-limitation prevails as the basis for liberty rights between the nineteenth and twentieth centuries.[50] Moreover, from this standpoint, even the subject of public order was addressed within the scope of police matters (Ranelletti 1904), with an approach in line with the Public Security Act elaborated by Francesco Crispi in 1889[51] and the Criminal Code of 1890, which was criticized by liberal-leaning constitutional lawyers (Arangio Ruiz 1898).

Aside from the universal nature and protection of liberty rights, the more rigid legal positivist approach which Arturo Rocco wished to impose on Italian criminal science (Rocco 1910), was increasingly prevalent. This approach "provided an objective way to give theoretical coverage to the authoritarian temptations of a crisis-inspired Liberal State, deeply concerned in safeguarding the *status quo*" (Fiandaca 2002, 33). The scope of the idea of public order in criminal and administrative law created a breeding ground for authoritarian use (and abuse) of the concept of public order by the Fascist dictatorship,

---

49 As a matter of fact, his 1905 work *Allgemeine Staatslehre* (Italian translation *La dottrina generale del diritto dello Stato*, Milano, Giuffrè, 1949) is not guided in a purely formal sense, for it highlights "the laborious reappearance of civil society in the area of dominant public law" (Lanchester 1985, 91). A more recent analysis can be found in Ridola (2016).

50 This approach, defended in particular by Oreste Ranelletti, was not followed by liberal constitutionalists like Arcoleo (1907), Racioppi and Brunelli (1909) or Arangio Ruiz (1913).

51 On this point, see the contributions of Barile et al. (1967).

limiting and annulling freedom in Italy (Neumann 1963). Not in vain were the theses contained in Gerber's work of 1852, in contrast to those of Jellinek, taken up by Orlando, reassessed in authoritarian systems. In fact, Jellinek's theory of the existence and nature of "subjective public rights", despite its centralist State connotations, had more liberal evocations among its aims, according to which the citizen's public rights were mere "reflex effects" or "reflex rights" of the monarch's power (von Gerber).[52]

To this regard, Carlo Costamagna's stance in "voce constitutionalis" (included in the Dictionary of Politics, edited by the National Fascist Party), is relevant. The author states that "there was no longer a place in Italy for a theory of subjective public rights", nor for liberty rights or a misconception of the separation of powers (Galizia 2013, 96).

As we know, the inviolable human rights will go on to have full recognition and protection in the democratic constitutions of the post–World War II period. These constitutions are established as the basis of political legitimacy, and so, are not subject to constitutional review: they are the *memory* and *future* of constitutions and of constitutionalism.

References

Arangio Ruiz, G (1898) *Storia costituzionale d'Italia (1848–1898)*. Civelli, Firenze.
Arangio Ruiz, G (1913) *Istituzioni di diritto costituzionale italiano*. Bocca, Torino.
Azzariti, G (2011) Il liberalismo autoritario e la costruzione dello Stato unitario italiano. Vittorio Emanuele Orlando, Un liberale al servizio dello Stato. *Democrazia e diritto* 1(2): 117–134.
Bacot, G (1985) *Carré de Malberg et l'origine de la distinction entre souveraineté du peuple et souveraineté nationale*. Ed. C.N.R.S., Paris.
Barberis, M (1984) *Il liberalismo empirico di Benjamin Constant. Saggio di storiografia analítica*. Ecig, Genova.
Barberis, M (1988) *Benjamin Constant. Rivoluzione, costituzione, progresso*. Il Mulino, Bologna.
Barbier, M (1966) Introduction. In: Barbier, M, de Vitoria, F (eds) *Leçon sur les Indiens et le droit de guerre*. Librairie Droz, Genève.
Barile, P (ed) (1967) *Pubblica sicurezza*, Proceedings of Conference commemorating the centenary of the administrative laws of unification (Firenze, 1965). Neri Pozza, Vicenza.
Bastid, P (1966) *Benjamin Constant et sa doctrine*. Librairie Armand Colin, Paris.
Bobbio, N (1963) *Locke e il diritto naturale*. Giappichelli, Torino.
Bonfiglio, S (2009) Fra antica costituzione e costituzionalismo moderno. In: *Petition of Right [1628]*. Liberilibri, Macerata.

---

52 On the contrary, as we have already said, in the *Grundzüge* there is indeed a liberal conception of the State.

Boudon, J (2012) Ingérence, conquête, annexion, réunion rattachement. Les mots de la Révolution française. *Droits* 56: 97–98.

Buratti, A (2012) *Veti presidenziali. Presidenti e maggioranze nell'esperienza costituzionale statunitense*. Carocci, Roma.

Casalini, B (2005) L'esprit di Montesquieu negli Stati Uniti (secolo XVIII). In: Felice, D (ed) *Montesquieu e i suoi interpreti*. Edizioni ETS, Pisa.

Cassese, S (2011) Auf der gefahrenvollen Strasse des öffentlichen Rechts. La "rivoluzione scientifica" di Vittorio Emanule Orlando. *Materiali per una storia della cultura giuridica* 2: 310–ff.

Cerroni, U (1979) *Princìpi di política*. Editori Riuniti, Rome.

Conklin, W.E (1979) *In Defence of Fundamental Rights*. Sijthoff & Noordhoff, Alphen aan den Rijn & Germantown.

Constant, B (1819) The Liberty of Ancients Compared with That of Moderns. Italian edition: Paoletti, G (ed) (2005) *La libertà degli antichi, paragonata a quella dei moderni*. Einaudi, Torino.

Cotta, S (1953) *Montesquieu e la scienza della società*. Ramella, Turin.

Cuoco, V (1801) *Saggio storico sulla rivoluzione napoletana del 1799*. In: De Francesco, A (ed) (2014) Saggio storico sulla rivoluzione di Napoli. Laterza, Roma-Bari.

De Luca, S (1993) *Il pensiero politico di Benjamin Constant*, Laterza, Roma-Bari.

De Luca, S (2003) *Alle origini del liberalismo contemporaneo. Il pensiero di Benjamin Constant tra il Termidoro e l'Impero*. Marco Editore, Lungro di Cosenza.

Desmos, E (2012) Illustration d'une manie française. Le "devoir d'ingérence" sous la Deuxième République. *Droits* 56: 129–130.

De Tocqueville, A (1856) L'Ancien Régime et la Révolution. English edition: Bonner, J (2017) *The Old Regime and the Revolution*. Harper & Brothers, New York. Available via http://oll.libertyfund.org/titles/2419 Accessed 2 February 2017.

De Vitoria, F. (1532) De Indis. Bilingual edition: Pereña, L, Pérez Prendes, J.M et al. (1967) *Relectio de Indis o Libertad de los Indios Consejo Superior de Investigaciones Científicas*. CSIC, Madrid.

Dicey, A.V (1885) *Introduction to the Study of the Law of the Constitution*. Available via http://files.libertyfund.org/files/1714/0125_Bk.pdf Accessed 2 February 2017.

Engels, F (1878) *Anti-Dühring*. In Marx-Engels Opere, Vol. 25 (1974). Editori Riuniti, Roma.

Felice, D (ed) (1998) *Leggere l'Esprit des Lois. Stato, società e storia nel pensiero di Montesquieu*. Liguori Editore, Napoli.

Felice, D (2014) *Montesquieu. Tutte le opere (1721–1754)*. Bompiani, Milano.

Fiandaca, G, Musco, E (2002) *Diritto penale. Parte generale*. Bologna, Zanichelli.

Galizia, M (1951) *La teoria della sovranità dal Medio Evo alla Rivoluzione francese*. Giuffrè, Milano.

Galizia, M (ed) (2013) *Appunti sugli anni della guerra di Paolo Galizia (1923–1944)*. Giuffrè, Milano.

Gerber, K. F (1852) *Über öffentliche Rechte*. Italian edition: Lucchini, P. L (ed) (1971) *Sui diritti pubblici*. In: *Diritto pubblico*, Giuffrè, Milano.

Gerber, K. F (1865) *Grundzüge des deutschen Staatssrechts*, Italian edition: Lucchini, P. L (ed) (1971) *Lineamenti di diritto pubblico tedesco*. In: *Diritto pubblico*, Giuffrè, Milano.

Gómez Robledo, A (1940) *Política de Vitoria*. Imprenta Universitaria, México.

Gramsci, A (1975) Quaderni del carcere. In Fubini, E (ed) *Sul Risorgimento o.* Editori Riuniti. Roma.

Heller, H (1929) Observations on the Problem of Contemporary Theory of State and of Law. In: Pasquino, P (ed) (1987) *La sovranità ed altri scritti sulla dottrina del diritto e dello Stato.* Giuffrè, Milano.

Hobbes, T (1651) *Leviathan.* Italian edition: Santi, R. (ed) (2001) *Leviatano.* Bompiani, Milano.

Jellinek, G (1895) *The Declaration of the Rights of Man and of Citizens: A Contribution to Modern Constitutional History.* Available via http://oll.libertyfund. org/titles/jellinek-the-declaration-of-the-rights-of-man-and-of-citizens Accessed 2 February 2017.

Jellinek, G (1901) *The Declaration of the Rights of Man and of Citizens: A Contribution to Modern Constitutional History.* Henry Holt and Company, New York. Italian edition: (2002) *La dichiarazione dei diritti dell'uomo e del Cittadino.* Giuffrè, Milano.

Lanchester, F (1985) *Alle origini di Weimar. Il dibattito costituzionalistico tedesco fra il 1900 e il 1918.* Giuffrè, Milano.

Locke, J (1689a) A Letter Concerning Toleration. Italian edition: Viano, C.A (ed) (2008) *Lettera sulla tolleranza.* In *Annex Saggio sulla tolleranza.* Laterza, Roma-Bari.

Locke, J (1689b) *A Letter Concerning Toleration* (trans: Popple, W). Available via Constitution Society www.constitution.org/jl/tolerati.htm Accessed 30 January 2017.

Locke, J (1690) Second Treatise on Government. Italian edition: Firpo, L (ed) (1982) *Due trattati sul governo.* In: *Classici della politica,* 3rd edn. Utet, Torino.

Martinelli, C (2014) *Diritto e diritti oltre la Manica. Perché gli inglesi amano tanto il loro sistema giuridico.* Il Mulino, Bologna.

Marx, K (1843) *On the Jewish Question.* Available via Marx & Engel's Library www. marxists.org/archive/marx/works/1844/jewish-question/ Accessed 2 February 2017.

Marx, K (1844a) *A Contribution to the Critique of Hegel's Philosophy of Right.* Available via Marx & Engel's Library www.marxists.org/archive/marx/works/1843/ critique-hpr/intro.htm Accessed 2 February 2017.

Marx, K (1844b) A Contribution to the Critique of Hegel's Philosophy of Right. Italian edition: Della Volpe, G (ed) (1969) *Critica della filosofia hegeliana del diritto pubblico.* In: *Opere filosofiche giovanili,* 4th edn. Editori Riuniti, Rome.

Mattei, U (2014) *Il modello di Common Law,* 4th edn. Giappichelli, Torino.

Matteucci, N (1976) *Organizzazione del potere e libertà.* Utet, Torino.

Matteucci, N (1992) Costituzionalismo. In: *Enciclopedia delle scienze sociali.* Available via Treccani www.treccani.it/ Accessed 3 February 2017.

McIlwain, C.H (1923) *The American Revolution: A Constitutional Interpretation.* The Macmillan Company, New York. Italian edition: (1965) *La Rivoluzione Americana: un'interpretazione costituzionale.* Mulino, Bologna.

Milazzo, L (2012) *La teoria dei diritti di Francisco de Vitoria.* Edizioni ETS, Pisa.

Moccia, L (2001) Modelli di tutela dei privati verso le pubbliche amministrazioni nella comparazione "civil law-common law": l'esperienza inglese. In: Picardi, N Sassani, B et al. (ed) *Diritto e processo, in memory of Alessandro Giuliani.* E.S.I., Napoli.

Modugno, F (1966) *Poteri (Divisione dei).* In: *Nss. D.I,* Vol. XIII, Utet, Torino.

Montesquieu Ch. de Secondat (1748) *De l'esprit des lois*. Italian edition: Felice, D. (ed) (2014) *Montesquieu. Tutte le opere (1721–1754)*. Bompiani, Milano.

Morelli, A (1898) La prima cattedra di diritto costituzionale. In: *Archivio giuridico* "Filippo Serafini", vol. 1, *Fava e Garagnani*, Bologna-Modena.

Mortati, C (1986) Dottrine generali e Costituzione della Repubblica italiana. In: *Enciclopedia del diritto*, vol. 11. Giuffrè, Milano.

Naszályi, P.E (1948) *El Estado según Francisco de Vitoria* (trans Menéndez-Reigada, I). Ediciones Cultura Hispánica, Madrid.

Neumann, F (1963) *Lo Stato Democratico e lo Stato autoritario*. Il Mulino, Bologna.

Nigro, M (1973) *Il "segreto" di Gerber*. In: *Quaderni fiorentini*, Vol. 2. Giuffrè, Milano.

Oestreich, G (2001) *La storia dei diritti umani e delle libertà fondamentali*. Laterza, Roma-Bari.

Orlando, V.E (1886) Studi giuridici sul governo parlamentare. In: *Archivio giuridico* "Filippo Serafini", Vol. 36, *Fava e Garagnani*, Bologna-Modena.

Orlando, V.E (1889) I criteri tecnici per la ricostruzione giuridica del diritto pubblico. In: *Archivio Giuridico* "Filippo Serafini", vol. 42. *Fava e Garagnani*, Bologna-Modena.

Orlando, V.E (1912) Sulla teoria dei "diritti pubblici subiettivi" di Jellinek. In: Orlando, V.E (1954) *Scritti Varii (1881–1940) Diritto Pubblico Generale*. Giuffrè, Milano.

Pérez Luño, A.E (2010) *Derechos humanos, estado de derecho y Constitución*, 5th edn. Tecnos, Madrid.

Pettit, P (1997) *Republicanism: A Theory of Freedom and Government*. Clarendon Press, Oxford.

Pinkard, T (2014) *La filosofia tedesca 1760–1860. L'eredità dell'idealismo*. Einaudi, Torino.

Pocock, J.G.A (1975) *The Machiavellian Moment: Fiorentine Political Throught and the Atlantic Republican Tradition*. Princeton University Press, Princeton.

Racioppi, F, Brunelli, I (1909) *Commento allo Statuto del Regno*, vol. II. Unione tipografico-editrice, Torino.

Ranelletti, O (1904) La polizia di sicurezza. In: Orlando V.E (ed) *Trattato completo di diritto ammistrativo italiano*, vol. 4. Società Editrice Libraria, Milano.

Ridola, P (2016) *Stato e Costituzione in Germania*. Giappichelli, Torino.

Rinella, A (2008) La Carta della Rivoluzione americana, in Dichiarazione di Indipendenza degli Stati Uniti d'America. In: *Il Monitore Costituzionale*. Liberilibri, Macerata.

Rocco, A (1910) Il problema e il metodo della scienza del diritto penale (Criminal Law and Procedure lectures January 1910, University of Sassari). *Riv. it. dir. pen.*

Rossi, P (1866) *Cours de droit constitutionnel*. Paris.

Rousseau J.J (1765) *Constitutional Project for Corsica*. Available via Constitution Society www.constitution.org/jl/tolerati.htm Accessed 30 January 2017.

Rousseau, J.J (1772a) *Considerations on the Government of Poland and on Its Proposed Reformation*. Available via Constitution Society www.constitution.org/jl/tolerati.htm Accessed 30 January 2017.

Rousseau, J.J (1772b) Considerations on the Government of Poland and on Its Proposed Reformation. Italian edition: Gherardi, R (ed) *Considerazioni sul governo di Polonia e sulla sua progettata riforma (1770–1771)*. In: Gherardi, R (ed) (2002) *Relazioni fra gli stati: pace e guerra. Forma di governo e sistema economico dall'illuminismo all'imperialismo*. Clueb, Bologna.

Rousseau, J.J (1972c) In: Rossi, P (ed) *Opere*. Sansoni Editore, Firenze.

Sabine, G.H (1981) *Storia delle dottrine politiche*, 2nd edn. Universale Etas, Milano.

Sacco, R.I (1991) Modelli notevoli di società. In Monateri, P.G, Mattei, U (eds) *Cardozo Lectures in Law*. Cedam, Padova.

Savigny, F.C (1814) *Vom Beruf unserer Zeit für Gesetzgebung und Rechtswissenschaft*. Italian edition: Thibaut, A.F.J, Von Savigny, F.C *La vocazione del nostro secolo per la legislazione e la giurisprudenza*. In: Marini, G (ed) (1982) *La polemica sulla codificazione*. E.S.I., Napoli.

Scott, J.B (1939) *Law, the State, and the International Community, vol. II: Extracts Illustrating the Growth of Theories and Principles of Jurisprudence, Government, and the Law of Nations*. Columbia University Press, New York.

Silvestri, G (1984) *La separazione dei poteri*, vol. II. Giuffrè, Milano.

Skinner, Q (1998) *Liberty Before Liberalism*. Cambridge University Press, Cambridge.

Staël-Holstein, G (1818/1862) *Considérations sur la Révolution française*. Charpentier, Libraire-Éditeur, Paris.

Stanlis, P.J (2009) *Edmund Burke and Natural Law*. With a new introduction by V. Bradley Lewis. Transaction Publishers, New Brunswick.

Torre, A (ed) (2007) Magna Carta [1215]. Liberilibri.

Truyol Serra, A (1946) *The Principles of Political and International Law in the Work of Francisco de Vitoria*. Ediciones Cultura Hispánica, Madrid.

Tuck, R (1981) *Natural Rights Theories: Their Origin and Development*. Cambridge University Press, Cambridge.

Viano, C.A (2005) L'individualismo introvabile e la teoria lockiana della tolleranza. In: Chiodi, G.M, Gatti, R (ed) *La filosofia politica di Locke*. FrancoAngeli, Milano.

Vidal, E (1950) *Saggio sul Montesquieu*. Giuffré, Milano.

Wilhelm, W. (1958) Zur juristischen Methodenlehre im 19. Jahrhundert. Italian edition: Lucchini, P.L (ed) (1974) *Metodologia giuridica nel secolo XIX*. Giuffrè, Milano.

Part II

Fundamental rights and constitutional interpretation

2 Principles and fundamental rights as the foundation of constitutional legal orders

2.1 Supremacy of constitutions and the prevalence of the fundamental principles they portray

Dictatorial and totalitarian regimes established in Europe within the first decades of the twentieth century denied the concept of the individual as an end unto him- or herself, reducing the person to a simple means to an end. In other words, they disregarded the Kantian imperative of the idea of human dignity.

It is no accident that the Preamble of the post–World War II German constitution, the Bavarian Constitution of 1946, condemned the utter devastation caused by "an order devoid of God, without conscience and without respect for the dignity of man".[1]

It was only after World War II that the true turning point came: the very rationale (*ratio*) of international standards for the protection of human rights changed, viewing the individual as an object of protection solely because of his or her intrinsic worth as a person. In addition, the foundations of democratic constitutionalism were finally consolidated. Lack of such consolidation after World War I had led to the advent of Fascism in Italy, the tragic end of the Weimar Republic in Germany and the Spanish Civil War.

In order to avoid repeating past horrors and mistakes, most European democratic constitutions of the post–World War II period – some of which even recognize a right of resistance[2] – approach State power as an

---

1 This is the Kantian principle stated in the *Groundwork of the Metaphysic of Morals* of 1785, which appeared a few years before the French Declaration of the Rights of Man and the Citizen (1789) and was confirmed in *The Metaphysics of Customs,* published in two parts in 1797.

2 The Fundamental Law of the Federal Republic of Germany is a good example, for it states: "all Germans shall have the right to resist any person seeking to abolish this constitutional

instrument for the recognition and protection of the dignity of the person and that person's inviolable, inalienable human rights.

Under this approach, constitutional democracies cannot be reduced simply to a method of electing political leaders, nor to mere government legitimation processes (Schumpeter 1942, 257). Therein, regulatory principles, which are embodied in the respect of the forms and limits set forth in the constitutions themselves, have a special link with both the 'structural principles' (*Strukturprinzipien*), among which is the democratic principle, and also with the 'constitutional principles' (*Verfassungprinzip*), from which programmatic norms, which deal with the dynamics of the legal order, are derived. Without this, democracies devoid of principles and values would be empty shells, deprived of content: procedures would have no normative basis. Without 'form or limits', democracies would degenerate into ochlocracies, into old authoritarian and plebiscitarian forms, or into new forms of populism.

Lawyers faced with the supremacy of constitutions must recognize the pre-eminence of the fundamental principles that characterize them. This pre-eminence is confirmed through the recognition of the formal (procedural) and material (substantive) limits on the power of constitutional review.

2.2 Fundamental rights and limits to the power of constitutional review: a comparison of experiences

The Italian Constitution establishes three explicit limits to the power of constitutional review: the "republican form" of government (Article 139); the inviolable human right to develop unhindered, in individual and collective contexts (Article 2); and an explicit procedural limit on the merger of existing Regions or the creation of new Regions (Article 132.1).[3]

---

order, if no other remedy is available" (Article 20.4 BL). Even before the constitution, which included the aforementioned article, certain constitutions of the *Länder* already recognized the right of resistance: the constitution of the free city of Bremen (Article 19); the constitution of Brandenburg Land of 1947 (Article 6); the Hessian Constitution of 1947 (Article 147); and the constitution of the city of Berlin of 1950 (Article 23.3). In addition, the right of resistance has been recognized in other constitutions adopted after the fall of dictatorial regimes: the constitution of the Greek Republic of 1975 (Article 120.4) and the Portuguese Constitution of 1976 (Article 21). In Italy, the proposal to explicitly include this right in the constitutional text was presented to Parliament by Dossetti, but was not approved.

3 A merger between existing Regions or the creation of new Regions having a minimum of one million inhabitants may be agreed when such request has been made by a number of Municipal Councils, representing no less than one-third of the populations involved, and when the request has been approved by referendum by a majority of said populations.

The republican form of government agreed by referendum[4] and closely linked to the principle of democracy (Article 1) constitutes a positive, though implicit, foundation of both constitutional case law[5] and doctrine.[6] Both have, on numerous occasions, highlighted the existence of other implicit limits to constitutional review, especially the non-availability of 'supreme principles' by the established powers.

Should any of these principles be violated, the Italian Constitutional Court can invalidate even lawful legislation and make its position prevail over that of the body in charge of the constitutional review. According to the aforementioned ruling, the Constitutional Court has attributed this power to itself.

In the Federal Republic of Germany, the Basic Law (BL) is very clear on the question of absolute limits to constitutional review.

Following the Preamble, Article 1 of the BL establishes the respect and protection of the dignity of the person,[7] as a supreme value that cannot be restricted; the recognition of "inviolable and inalienable human rights"; and in addition, establishes that fundamental rights "are binding on legislature, executive, and judiciary as directly valid [applicable] law". More specifically, the BL itself establishes absolute limits to constitutional review: any modification that may affect fundamental rights or the division of the federal State in *Länder* and, likewise, their participation in the legislative procedure is not admissible (Article 79.3 BL).

Unlike the Italian and German constitutions, the Spanish Constitution[8] is much more 'rigid', in the strict sense of the term, considering the complexity of the constitutional review procedure, though it does not set an absolute limit to such revision. The Spanish Constitution provides for a partial review procedure, in addition to another specially qualified procedure (the so-called aggravated procedure)[9] in cases where there is a 'total' revision or

---

4 For more on the unavailability of the republican form of government in the constituent assembly, see Pinelli (1981, 88).

5 See Italian Constitutional Court, judgement n.1146/1988.

6 On this point, see, among others see Mortati (1952), Grossi (1972) and more recently, De Martino (2014) and Bonfiglio (2015).

7 In accordance with Federal Constitutional Court case law and Günther Dürig's theory, the constitution is a hierarchy of values, the highest of which is human dignity, as provided therein.

8 See among others: (García Pelayo 1984; de Vega 1988; Pérez Royo 1987; Blanco Valdés 2006).

9 The aggravated procedure is not easy to apply because of what is needed for approval to proceed with the reform: (a) the majority of two-thirds of both Houses; (b) the subsequent dissolution of the Spanish Parliament (Cortes); (c) the Houses elected therein must ratify the decision and proceed to examine the new constitutional text, which must be passed by a

when it affects fundamental rights and public freedoms, which are given a reinforced protection (Pérez Luño 2007, 69).

In light of the Spanish experience, the first partial review procedure confirms both the rigidity of the procedure and infers the possibility of amending the Constitution (López Aguilar 2012, 199). The second procedure, incidentally, corroborates the rigidity of the review procedure but also the unchangeable tendency of the principles and fundamental rights, regulated in Articles 14 to 29, (which the Constitution permits to develop organically), in addition to the *amparo* appeal in case of alleged violations.

On the other hand, in confirming the unchangeable nature of fundamental principles and rights, Spanish theory and case law (Muñoz Machado 2006, 459) have both indicated material, sometimes conflicting limits on constitutional (and even supra-constitutional) power. These limits stem from certain judgements made by the Spanish Constitutional Court in relation to political parties, whose functioning must conform to democratic principles.[10]

This point of view was most recently confirmed by Judgement 42/2014, in which the Constitutional Court declared the Declaration on the

---

two-thirds majority of the members of each House; and (d) once the reform is approved, it must be submitted to a referendum for approval (Article 168). If the referendum is mandatory, in the case of a partial revision, the referendum must be requested by a tenth of the members of one of the two Chambers, within 15 days after the approval of the reform (Article 167.3). In the absence of such requirement, for the two reforms so far adopted through the procedure established in Article 167, the referendum has not been used. The first constitutional amendment procedure dates back to 27 August 1992, when Article 13 of the constitution, regulating the right of foreigners to vote, was modified to include the words "and the right to be elected" in paragraph 2 of the above-mentioned provision ("Only Spaniards shall have the rights recognized in Article 23, except in cases which may be established by treaty or by law concerning the right to vote and the right to be elected in municipal elections, and subject to the principle of reciprocity"). The second constitutional amendment procedure modified Article 135 of the constitution to include the principle of budgetary stability, whose entry by force occurred on 27 September 2011.

Translator's note: the so-called aggravated constitutional amendment procedure is a special qualified procedure, requiring a qualified majority and other equally qualified conditions, making it different from the "ordinary" legislative procedure, requiring simple majority. Hence, the so-called aggravated procedure and specially qualified procedure will be used interchangeably.

10 See Constitutional Court Judgement 48/2003 of 12 March ruling on the constitutional legitimacy of the Organic Law governing political parties, which refers to the constitutional principles that "bind, as does the Constitution, citizens and public powers (Article 9.1 SC), even when its review or amendment is postponed and until it is not successfully verified through the procedures established in its Title X". Likewise, in the same judgement, the Constitutional Court adds that "any project is compatible with the Constitution, provided it is not defended through an activity that violates democratic principles or fundamental rights".

Sovereignty and the right to decide of the people of Catalonia and the unilateral call for a referendum on the independence (Barceló i Serramalera 2015) of the Autonomous Community to be unconstitutional. The Court found that such acts opposed the constitutional principles proclaimed in Articles 1.2 and 2 of the Constitution, which recognized the unity of the Spanish nation and the Spanish people, attributing to the latter the exclusive ownership of national sovereignty. In the same judgement, the Court made a number of (arguably contradictory) interpretations, in relation to the procedural rules surrounding Catalan self-government, foreseen by the Constitution in judgement 32/2015 of 25 February 2015. The Court suspended Decree 129/2014 of the President of the Generalitat of Catalonia, concerning the call "of a non-referendary popular consultation"[11] on the political future of the Autonomous Community. In order to realise the aspirations of independence of the Catalan people, the autonomous Legislative Assembly, in accordance with the indications given in Judgement 42/2014, had two choices. It could either request that the government adopt a bill, or it could submit a legislative proposal (Article 87.2 and 166 SC) for the revision of the Constitution – through the so-called aggravated procedure of constitutional amendment, before the Presidency of the Spanish Congress of Deputies. Once the procedural limits of a "total review" were reached, this would remove any obstacle to Catalonia's right to self-proclaim itself sovereign.

To a certain degree, the Spanish Constitutional Court regards the so-called aggravated procedure as the guardian of the Constitution and its principles. However, the absence of explicit material limits and the purely textual (literal) interpretation of the rules on constitutional review can cause, such as in the Spanish case, a kind of short circuit. For instance, what would prevent the use of the procedure provided in Article 167 in order to modify Article 168's specially qualified (aggravated) procedure? Title X of the Constitution, dedicated to *Constitutional Reform*, is not even amongst the provisions whose modification requires approval through an 'aggravated' procedure. Arguably, in addition to recognizing some implicit material limits, any proposal for derogation, suspension or modification of

---

11 Not surprisingly, within the judgement of 25 February 2015, the Constitutional Court suspended Act 10/2014 of the Catalan Parliament that regulated – under the name "general consultations" – a popular vote, through which the autonomous legislature has ignored the consequences that derive from Articles 23.1 and 149.1.1 SC in relation to Article 81.1 SC, 92.3 SC and 149.1.32 SC, which attributes to the State an exclusive competence though not limited to state authorization in the case of convening popular consultations by referendum, does "extends to the entire institutional apparatus for its establishment and regulation" (STC 31/2010, of June 28, FJ 69).

the 'aggravated' procedure should be excluded, the latter being understood as the absolute procedural limit of constitutional amendment.

In addition to Spain, during the second half of the 1970s, two military dictatorships[12] fell in Western Europe: Portugal and Greece.

The Portuguese Constitution contains a long and detailed list of material limits to constitutional reform, among which are fundamental freedoms, rights and guarantees (Article 288.1.d). It also includes some circumstantial limits (Article 289): no amendment may be admitted during a state of siege or in a state of emergency. In addition, the Constitution permits revisions five years after the publication of the most recent ordinary law concerning its review (Article 284.1). This provision also provides that a review may be endorsed earlier, as long as it gains approval by a majority of four-fifths of the deputies (Article 284.2).

Likewise, the Greek Constitution (following amendments in 2001) extended its own fundamental rights protection and added material limits for its reform, including personal liberty (Article 5.3) and freedom of thought (Article 13. 1). The Greek Constitution, much like the Portuguese Constitution, also establishes temporary limits and foresees that the Constitution may be amended five years after its last revision (Article 110.6).

2.3 Subsequent elements to legal comparison

Explicit references to formal and material limits of constitutional amendment are also evident in the constitutions of Eastern European States which, following the fall of the Berlin Wall,[13] ratified the European Convention on Human Rights (ECHR) and became members of the European Union.

Both Czechoslovakia's and the later Czech Republic's constitutional experiences are exemplary and represent a clear break with a communist past.[14] Regarding the former, before the adoption of the Constitution, the Federal Assembly, on 9 January 1991, adopted the Charter of Fundamental Rights and Freedoms, enacted as constitutional statute. In its Article 1.1 the "supra-constitutional" nature of the Charter is established, providing that constitutional statutes, other statutes and legal acts, as well as their interpretation and application, must be in accordance with the Charter of Fundamental Rights and Freedoms (Di Gregorio 2008). The Constitution situation

---

12 On this point, see, among others De Vergottini (1977) and Kaminis (1993).
13 On this point, see, among others Vergottini (1998), Lanchester and Ragionieri (1998), Linz and Stepan (2000), and Ganino (2002, 2003).
14 On this point, see, among others Knapp and Bartole (1994).

itself, in its Article 3, establishes the Charter – where other constitutional principles are set out – as an integral part of the constitutional system.[15]

The Constitution of the Czech Republic, which came into effect on 1 January 1993, may be supplemented or amended only by statutes of constitutional rank (Article 9.1). But modifying the essential principles of the democratic rule of law is forbidden (Article 9.2). Furthermore, the interpretation of its rules is no justification for undermining or endangering the foundations of a democratic State (Article 9.3). According to scholars and constitutional case law, the principles contained in Chapter I of the Constitution (separation of powers, origin and constitutional protection of human rights and freedoms and so forth) constitute an absolute limit to the constitutional amendment procedure. According to the Constitutional Court, the basic requirements of a democratic State governed by the rule of law are located outside the tasks of the constitutional legislator.

The Slovak Republic was born out of the peaceful split of Czechoslovakia. In 1992, the Slovak Constitution was adopted, and subsequently amended on several occasions,[16] even though a majority of three-fifths of the members of Parliament is necessary for its review (Article 84. 4). A referendum is not needed in order to pass constitutional legislation, except in cases where the entry or exit of a union of states is decided, as provided in Articles 7.1 and 93.1. The Constitution prohibits the use of the referendum when it concerns fundamental rights and freedoms, as well as taxes, levies and State budget (Article 93.3). Fundamental rights and freedoms have special recognition and protection, since they are inalienable, imprescriptible and inviolable (Article 12). Along these same lines, the principle of political pluralism, without any ideological or religious link (Article 1.1), the right of resistance,[17] the rights of national minorities and ethnic groups (Article 33), political movements and parties (Articles 29.2 and 29.4) and the suspension of political rights (Article 29.3), as well as the unrestricted participation of political actors in a democratic society (Article 31) and their control by the Constitutional Court (Article 129.4) all have a similar status.

In Poland, we find another relevant example. The Polish Constitution[18] was adopted in 1997, recalling "the bitter experiences of the times when

15 For a deeper analysis, see http://spcp.prf.cuni.cz/aj/2-93en.htm.
16 English version can be found on the Czech Republic Parliament's website.
17 Article 32 of its constitution provides: "Citizens have the right to put up resistance against anyone who would eliminate the democratic order of basic human rights and freedoms listed in this constitution, if the activity of constitutional bodies and the effective use of legal means are rendered impossible".
18 For more information regarding the Polish constitutional transition see, among others, De Martin, Gambale et al. (2007), Filippini (2010), Policastro (2003).

fundamental freedoms and human rights were violated in our homeland" in its Preamble. Among the general principles laid forth in the Constitution, there is a reference to inherent and inalienable human dignity, which is the origin of freedom, human rights and the rights of citizens. Dignity is thus inviolable, and its defence is the public authorities' duty (Article 30). In addition to the so-called aggravated procedure, the Polish Constitution also has a specially qualified procedure (Articles 235.5 and 235.6), if constitutional amendments apply to Chapters I (republic), II (rights, freedoms and duties of the person and the citizen) and XII (constitutional review).

Take the Romanian Constitution, which also[19] provides a special procedure for constitutional reform, specifying the material and circumstantial limits of the amendment itself (during a state of siege or emergency or even during times of war).[20]

Article 152 (paragraphs 1 and 2) of the Romanian Constitution sets out the limits of the constitutional amendment procedure: the national, independent, unitary and indivisible nature of the Romanian State; the republican form of government; territorial integrity; judicial independence; political pluralism; the official language; and the rights, freedoms and guarantees of citizens.

19 According to the amended text, included by Constitutional Reform Act 429/2003, published in the *Official Gazette,* Part I, number 758, 29 October 2003. This law, approved by national referendum on 18 and 19 October 2003, entered into force on 29 October 2003, in accordance with the decision of the Constitutional Court confirming the result of the national referendum. The text of the constitution, translated into English and French, can be found on the website of the Romanian Constitutional Court. The constitutional amendment procedure modified 62, eliminated 5 and added 9 additional articles. The aims of the reform can be summarized as follows: increased institutional and constitutional guarantees as regards fundamental rights and freedoms, and compliance with the constitutional constraints required for the integration of Romania into the European Union and accession to NATO.

20 With regard to the constitutions analyzed, the most important difference is the power of initiative held not only by the Romanian president, at the proposal of the government or at least one-fourth of the deputies or senators, but also by a minimum of 500,000 citizens with voting rights (Article 150.1). Citizens who initiate the constitutional amendment procedure must come from at least half of the provinces of the country. In each of these provinces (or from the Municipality of Bucharest) at least 20,000 signatures supporting this initiative must be registered (Article 150. 2). For the adoption of the draft reform, a qualified majority voting is envisaged: (a) a majority of at least two-thirds of the number of members of each House (Article 151.1); (b) if, by means of the mediation procedure, no agreement is reached, the Congress of Deputies and the Senate, in a joint session, decide by a vote of at least three-quarters of the both combined (Article 151.2). However, referendum is mandatory: the amendment procedure is final only after its approval by popular referendum, organized within a maximum period of 30 days from the date of approval of the project or the proposal for constitutional review (Article 151.3).

2.4 Stability and foundation of constitutional systems

What conclusions, then, can be drawn from this brief review of the explicit and implicit limits to the constitutional amendment procedure in written constitutions?

1 The adoption of a specially qualified ('aggravated') procedure of constitutional amendment is established as a general and functional governing principle, with respect to the preservation or 'maintenance' of the written constitution, and as an instrumental principle with respect to democratic and other fundamental principles enshrined in the constitutional order.
2 Any total amendment procedure must comply with the constitutional principles on the State form, in accordance with the current legal order. *Procedural constitutional principles*, although not specified, constitute real limits to constitutional reform and always include the inviolable rights of the person.
3 Constitutions can enable, and simultaneously prohibit, the amendment of certain parts (fundamental rights and principles), which confirms the so-called rigidity (in a strict or technical sense) of the written constitution.[21]
4 Stability or constitutional changes, however, depend less on *rigidity* than on the *structure* or the *foundation* of the constitutional order.

This last point also explains the stable basis for unwritten constitutions. According to Bryce, it would be a mistake "to pronounce Flexible Constitutions unstable. Their true note, their distinctive merit, is to be elastic. They can be stretched or bent so as to meet emergencies, without breaking their framework" (Bryce 1901, 25). Therefore, the concepts of flexibility and elasticity have a different meaning. The former explains purely formal changes, while the concept of 'elasticity' in a constitution emphasizes the stability of certain fundamental principles that refer to 'substantially constitutional provisions'.[22] Here, we can witness a strong theoretical influence due to the link between the notion of constitution and substantially constitutional principles.[23]

21 Bryce holds that "The essential fact is that in States with more modern constitutions, the higher or fundamental law, called Constitution, is placed over ordinary legislation and cannot be modified by the ordinary legislative power" (Bryce 1901, 10).
22 Suffice to mention the Albertine Statute and the notion of 'elasticity' that was used in the debates concerning the forms of government during the statutory period and, in particular, on the growing reforms of the fascist regime (Rossi 1940, 30–31; Mortati 1940; Bonfiglio 1993, 41).
23 On this point, see Lanchester (2011, 5) and Galizia (2013, 114).

So, it is not so surprising that a written constitution might actually prove more unstable and politically fragile than unwritten constitutions, consolidated in time and space as *historical constitutions* and reinforced by historical events and principles. The perfect example of this? The case of the English constitution. The 800th anniversary of the Magna Carta heralded some intense debate in the United Kingdom over the advantages and disadvantages of adopting a written constitution,[24] which later on might adopt a flexible nature within the limits of the fundamental principles that define the constitutional order.

Documentary constitutions have the advantage of being able to expressly provide programmed 'maintenance',[25] establishing, in some cases, precise formal (procedural) and relative and absolute material (substantive) limits that may impede the reform of "any of its parts".[26]

Subsequently, overcoming these insurmountable obstacles would lead to the creation of a new constitutional order, whose genesis – no longer dependent on the repeal of the procedural limits of the constitutional amendment procedure – would be set by the very fact of its overcoming.

If anti-constitutional political and social forces prevail over principles, norms and factual powers, this effectively eliminates the formal and material limits of constitutional amendment. Constituent power, though, is a *de facto* and not a *de jure* power.[27] As such, to consider a factual power, from a legal point of view, should only be on an *exceptional* basis. Constitutions are strengthened by history, reason and clear principles; care must also be taken as they are interpreted, evolve and are maintained to strengthen their foundations.

In his last work, Mario Galizia, criticizing Italian writers who sympathized with the Fascist regime, asserted that the constitution "must cling to 'constitutionalism' by integrating itself into its open and liberal cultural and historical dimension and by trying to dissuade any Jacobin element, linked to the precedent of political forces" (Galizia 2013, 95).

---

24 House of Commons – Political and Constitutional Reform Committee, *A new Magna Carta?*, Second Report of Session 2014–15, Ordered by the House of Commons to be printed on 3 July 2014 (www.publications.parliament.uk/pa/cm201415/cmselect/cmpolcon/463/463.pdf).

25 For example, Florida provides for a periodic review every 20 years, following a proposal from an express committee.

26 Some scholars, such as Guastini (1998, 1999, 114) believe that "anything [any part]" can be amended.

27 This thesis is widely accepted by General Theory constitutionalists and scholars. See, among others, Jellinek (1900), Kelsen (1945), Carré de Malberg (1922) and Schmitt (1928/1984).

The limits to the exercise of political authority, the balance between powers and the formal and material limits of procedure for constitutional amendment, must clearly appear in all (written or unwritten) constitutions, in order to underline what is an unbreakable link between constitutional theory and 'constitutionalism'; a link that economic globalization has cast doubt upon.

2.5 New trends and the weakening of constitutional principles: *global constitutionalism* and *societal constitutionalism*

In the previous liberal state crisis and in the current economic globalization, many scholars feel compelled to reconsider and criticize traditional legal categories attributable to statehood, and to question the effectiveness of the protection of fundamental rights in the context of cyclical economic and financial crises.

Since the *post-national constitutionalism* approach, renowned authors like Krisch (2010) have theorized about overcoming constitutionalism and even about a disappearance of the State, in the aftermath of an irreversible crisis. In this respect, an antithesis between constitutionalism and pluralism could inevitably arise.[28] However, the assumption this thesis is based upon is flawed: constitutionalism established on the basis of State monopoly, as opposed to pluralism that involves the recognition of diverse sources of authority, even from a normative aspect. Nonetheless, regional, federal and especially multicultural states clearly show a distinct pluralistic character based on the revaluation of diversity. In a sense, Krisch remains chained to the monistic conception of sovereignty and statehood that belongs to a nineteenth century interpretation of the law and the State. This is an anti-state position, both from a theoretical and ideological point of view, which seeks to maintain, in the name of pluralism, the primacy of politics above the rule of law. Such primacy, in his view, constitutes the true essence of *global constitutionalism*. Nonetheless, this summarized version of Krisch's rationale is questionable – given that it ignores the powerful impact of economic rules on (political) constitutions.

Indeed, in the last few decades, private multi-national corporations have grown and emerged as global sovereign subjects, capable of being direct and indirect rights manufacturers. To these large *corporations*, as global actors at times more powerful than most States, fundamental rights of individuals,

---

28 Unlike Krisch, Stone Sweet considered the contrast between constitutionalism, seen as a rigid hierarchy of social relations, and political pluralism, brought about by globalization as a forced comparison. See Stone Sweet (2013, 621) and, more recently, Amirante (2015).

groups and communities are no more than easily surmountable obstacles. One could even say that many States "collaborate" with these economic agents, liquidating "common goods", a form of fundamental rights (Mattei 2012, 7).

Another theoretical reflection, centered on relations between law and economy, is that of Teubner, noteworthy for its analytical and descriptive rigour.[29] In Teubner's works, the notions of 'constitution' and 'constitutionalism' are used to interpret the links between economics and the law, side-stepping contemporary constitutionalism and its principles. Instead, Teubner relies on spontaneous processes of self-regulation caused by sectoral interests and steered towards a constitutionalization of global economy, which encompasses corporate codes, conceived as "independent constitutions". Economics and the law are presented as two reciprocally closed systems that cannot form a single order, and so cannot be united in a single economic constitution. In fact, the meta-codes of transnational corporations claim hierarchical sovereignty over politics and law, incorporated in a constitutional code. According to Teubner, the processes of constitutionalization would have been separated anyway from the State, politics and constitutional principles altogether, whose survival passes through the incorporation of economical principles into legal norms. According to Teubner, this incorporation promotes a *re-entry* of the law in business organizations.

The theory of *societal constitutionalism*, according to which the "constitutions" of transnational corporations produce rules parallel to politically constitutional ones, is undoubtedly subject to important changes in its structure, processes and functions, shifting alongside the dynamics of worldwide scale economic undertakings. From this point of view, 'methodological nationalism' is not at all useful in highlighting these apparent trends. However, an anti-state ideological response, with a good dose of predominant methodological 'economism', might not apply to the reality of continental states – such as the United States, China, India and Russia – whose weight in the world at large is greater than that of the European Union (despite its economic and commercial strengths).

References

Amirante, A (2015) Al di là dell'Occidente. Sfide epistemologiche e spunti euristici nella comparazione "verso Oriente". *Diritto pubblico comparato ed europeo* 1.
Barceló i Serramalera, M (2015) Referendum e secessione. *La vicenda della Catalogna. Federalismi.it* 1.

---

29 See Teubner (2012 and 2014) and Ferrarese (2006).

Blanco Valdés, R (2006) *El valor de la Constitución. Separación de poderes, supremacía de la ley y control de constitucionalidad en los orígenes del Estado liberal*. Alianza, Madrid.

Bonfiglio, S (1993) *Forme di governo e partiti politici. Riflessioni sull'evoluzione della dottrina costituzionalistica italiana*. Giuffrè, Milano.

Bonfiglio, S (2015) Sulla rigidità delle Costituzioni. Il dibattito italiano e la prospettiva comparata. *Diritto pubblico* 1: 105–126.

Bryce, J (1901) Flexible and Rigid Constitutions. Italian edition: Pace, A (ed) (1998) *Costituzioni flessibili e rigide* (trans Niro, R). Giuffrè, Milano.

Carré de Malberg, R (1922) *Contribution à la théorie générale de l'Etat*. Sirey, Paris.

De Martin, G.C, Gambale, P et al. (eds) (2007) *Riforme costituzionali e itinerari della democrazia in Europa: Italia e Polonia a confronto*. Cedam, Padova.

De Martino, F.R (2014) *Le deroghe all'articolo 138 della Costituzione. L'esperienza repubblicana*. ESI, Napoli.

De Vega, P. (1988) *La reforma constitucional y la problemática del poder constituyente*. Tecnos, Madrid.

De Vergottini, G (1977) *Le origini della Seconda Repubblica Portoghese (1974/1976)*. Giuffré, Milano.

De Vergottini, G (1998) *Le transizioni costituzionali*. Il Mulino, Bologna.

Di Gregorio, A (2008) *Repubblica ceca*. Il Mulino, Bologna.

Ferrarese, M.R (2006) *Diritto sconfinato. Inventiva giuridica e spazi nel mondo globale*. Laterza, Roma-Bari.

Filippini, C (2010) *Polonia*. Il Mulino, Bologna.

Galizia, M (ed) (2013) Appunti sugli anni della guerra di Paolo Galizia (1923–1944). In: *Archivio di Storia Costituzionale e di Teoria della Costituzione*, vol. 8. Giuffrè, Milano.

Ganino, M (2002) Democrazia e diritti umani nelle Costituzioni dei Paesi dell'Europa orientale. In: Ganino, M, Venturini, G (eds) *L'Europa di domani: verso l'allargamento dell'Unione – Europe Tomorrow: Towards the Enlargement of the Union. Atti del Convegno*. Giuffrè, Milano.

García Pelayo, M. (1984) *Derecho constitucional comparado*. Alianza, Madrid.

Grossi, P.F (1972) *Introduzione ad uno studio sui diritti inviolabili nella Costituzione italiana*. Cedam, Padova.

Guastini, R (1999) La costituzione come limite alla legislazione. In: Comanducci, P, Guastini, R (eds) *Analisi e diritto 1998. Ricerche di giurisprudenza analitica*. Giappichelli, Torino.

Jellinek, G (1900) *Allgemeine Staatslehre*. Berlin. Italian edition: (1949) *La dottrina generale del diritto dello Stato*. Giuffrè, Milano.

Kaminis, G (1993) *La transition constitutionnelle en Grèce et en Espagne. Libr.* Générale de Droit et de Jurisprudence, Paris.

Kelsen, H (1945) *General Theory of Law and State*. Cambridge, MA. Italian edition: (1952) *Teoria generale del diritto e dello Stato*. Edizioni di Comunità, Milano.

Knapp, V, Bartole, S (eds) (1994) *La dissoluzione della Federazione cecoslovacca*. La Rosa editrice, Torino.

Krisch, N (2010) *Beyond Constitutionalism: The Pluralist Structure of Postnational Law*. Oxford University Press, Oxford.

Lanchester, F (2011) *La Costituzione tra elasticità e rottura*. Giuffrè, Milano.
Lanchester, F, Ragionieri, M.P (1998) *I successori dell'impero: le costituzioni degli ordinamenti ex URSS*. Giuffrè, Milano.
Linz, J.J, Stepan, A (2000) *L'Europa post-comunista*. Il Mulino, Bologna.
López Aguilar, J.F (2012) De la Constitución "irreformable" a la reforma constitucional "exprés". *Teoría y Realidad Constitucional* 29: 199–ff.
Mattei, U (2012) *Beni comuni. Un manifesto*. Laterza, Roma-Bari.
Mortati, C (1940) *La costituzione in senso materiale*. Giuffrè, Milano.
Mortati, C (1952) *Concetto, limiti, procedimento della revisione costituzionale*. Rivista trimestrale di diritto pubblico.
Muñoz Machado, S (2006) *Tratado de derecho administrativo y derecho público general*, vol. I. Justel, Madrid.
Pérez Luño, A.E (2007) *Los derechos Fundamentals*. Tecnos, Madrid.
Pérez Royo, J (1987) *La reforma de la Constitución*. Congreso de los Diputados, Madrid.
Pinelli, C (1981) *Costituzione rigida e costituzione flessibile nel pensiero dei costituenti italiani*. Giuffrè, Milano.
Policastro, P (2003) La transizione costituzionale polacca e l'Europa tra paradigmi del costituzionalismo e costituzionalismo multilivello. In: Gambino, S (ed) (2003) *Costituzionalismo europeo e transizioni democratiche*. Giuffrè, Milano.
Rossi, L (1940) La "elasticità" dello Statuto italiano. In: *Studi in onore di Santi Romano*, vol. I. Cedam, Padova.
Schmitt, C (1928) *Verfassungslehre*. Berlin. Italian edition: (1984) *Dottrina della costituzione*. Giuffrè, Milano.
Schumpeter, J.A (1942). Italian edition: (1964) *Capitalismo, socialismo, democrazia*. Edizioni di Comunità, Milano.
Stone Sweet, A (2013) The Structure of Constitutional Pluralism. In: *International Journal of Constitutional Law*. Yale Law School – Public Law Working Paper 291: 621–ff.
Teubner, G (2012) *Nuovi conflitti costituzionali. Norme fondamentali dei regimi transnazionali*. Bruno Mondadori, Milano.
Teubner, G (2014) *Ordinamento giuspubblicistico e società civile: doppia riflessività e metacodici ibridi*. VII Devolution Club Annual Seminar, March 2014.

3 Fundamental rights and the interpretative evolution of constitutional principles

3.1 Values, principles and interpretative canons

No human rights theory is self-sufficient. In addition to the generic universality of rights rhetoric, the limitation of powers and the guarantee of fundamental rights depend on the prescriptive force of constitutional principles. First and foremost, rights are interpreted, regulated and protected, in various areas, according to constitutional principles, since no *constitutionalism without principles* nor a *constitutionalism without rights* can in actual fact be conceived. For this reason, fundamental rights *must* bind all public authorities of the State in question "as a directly applicable right" (Article 1 of the Basic Law for the Federal Republic of Germany).

Hence, the interpretation and application of fundamental rights fall to the legislative, executive and judicial powers. However, the increasing importance of the judge's role in constitutional affairs is generating legal debate on the *juristocracy* (Hirschl 2004) and its activism. For example, in the United States, the Supreme Court has been criticized for its excessive activism, which, according to some voices, constitutes a threat to the founding principle (Tushnet 1999) of the American Constitution: "*We, the People*". Another extremely relevant case of activism is that of the Supreme Court of India. Through constitutional interpretation – and the frequent use of foreign precedents as the basis of its arguments, it has recognized rights not explicitly established therein.

Similarly, in Italy, the debate regarding constitutional courts started in the 1980s,[1] after the adoption of the most innovative social legislation in rela-

---

1 Previously, the emphasis was, in fact, placed on the constitution as a legal rule, in order to recognize the maximum binding nature of constitutional rules, and to confront the (conservative) attempt not to apply the constitution itself and to reduce certain constitutional provisions to mere declarations lacking legal force, in line with legal formalism (Barile 1951; Crisafulli 1952; Dogliani 1982; Zagrebelsky 1992, 153). In contrast, the normative

tion to the previous decade.[2] In the 1980s, Italian constitutionalists began to study the political weight of the Constitutional Court decisions more carefully, since it tended to exercise a supplementary role with regard to Parliament, developing a "political" role, through creative, quasi-legislative judgements.[3]

Since the 1990s, however, judicial activism has been considered excessive by those who wish to defend the political democracy of a *judicial dictatorship* (Quirk and Bridwell 1993), as a "guardian government" (Portinaro 1997, 434) and even, as Schmitt (1967) once put it, of a *tyranny of values*. This last criticism suggests a new interpretation of the political decision-making capacity, supporting the supremacy of 'political' as a new category, of State sovereignty, elections, exaltation of unity and homogeneity of citizens, in contrast to post-war democratic constitutionalism and the new plural European citizenship.

This position was famously coined by Schmitt, as a result of his profound aversion towards liberalism, democracy, the principle of separation of powers, the system of controls and guarantees, the balance between guiding principles, and mediation, all of which are essential in a complex, increasingly multicultural society. Even so, it is important to note that a judge cannot refuse to apply rules because they do not conform to his or her personal moral code: like every citizen they, too, are subject to the constitution.

To interpret any given provision, legal practitioners must use constitutional principles in the interest of their reasonable integration. Lawyers require principles as a reference, given that they are the institutional expression of values. Thus, principles are inherent to any legal activity, while values come under the broader sphere of public ethics.

Establishing a distinct separation between fundamental rights and values makes sure that there can be no *dictatorship of values* (or subjective discretion – in other words, arbitrariness – of any decision) on the party of judges, parliamentarians or political leaders: in the legal sphere, public authorities are legitimized by their compliance with constitutional principles.[4]

---

character of principles and programmatic norms enshrined in the constitution is confirmed by the case law, since the famous Constitutional Court judgement of 1956.

2 A period of social reforms were instigated in Italy in the early 1970s. In this context, the most significant studies pointed to the value of the law as a derivation of constitutional value, highlighting that constitutional legality "represents, in principle, a judgement on the correctness of such derivation and, in other words, observes that the legislation is, in fact, the continuation, development and is in accordance with the purpose of the Constitution" (Modugno 1970, 6).

3 On this point, see, among others Silvestri (1981), Ruggeri (1988) and Pegoraro (1987).

4 Silvestri (2009, 39) argues that "State bodies can (and should) ponder principles, which means that they must start with the positive data of constitutional dispositions, only referring

Adherence to principles reinforces the autonomy of the judiciary and their interpretation, and "restores" both the law's sociability and equity as its very essence.

The role of the judge, which traditionally consists of the interpretation of the law applied on a case-by-case basis, is, however, a "creative" activity, since it requires the interpretation of (legislative and *rational*) text as well as the complex context (to which the norm must be applied). A legal scholar's linguistic analysis cannot be solely the sum of legal science. Thus, the judge, taking into account that legal instruments are open to a multiplicity of meanings, must carry out a contextual analysis through certain interpretative techniques, an analysis which confirms the non-absolute and continuously evolving nature of fundamental rights.

Constitutional courts follow two main interpretive canons: reasonableness[5] and proportionality.[6] The first is used to measure the degree of conformity of the rule with constitutional principles and other related ordinary legislation, on a case-by-case basis. Reasonability is seen as "a criterion of protection enhancement and not as a minimum threshold of protection of the constitutional principles and fundamental rights at stake" (Silvestri 2009, 118). Proportionality *sensu stricto*, especially in cases involving fundamental rights,[7] comprises a test of the effects of the legislative act, comparing the benefits arising from the pursuit of the objective sought by the legislator and the negative effects to the rights and interests at stake (the measure should not be inconsistent with the objective). The principle of proportionality, broadly developed by the German Constitutional Court, is now a global constitutional (interpretative) model (Stone Sweet and Mathews 2008, 68–147) that is regularly employed by some of the world's most influential constitutional judges.

---

to values as a way to acquire a better understanding of the principles current content, when endlessly working in the adaptation of Law to social reality".

5 The principle of reasonableness, rooted in case law, has taken on very different meanings. In its first stage, the 'reasonableness' test in the Italian experience was linked to the principle of equality (see Cheli 2011, 7–40; 2015, 289–301). As can be seen, the principle of reasonableness is linked to the principle of proportionality so as to evaluate the adequacy of rules with respect to the facts that must be regulated. (Penasa 2009, 817).

6 The principle of proportionality has its origins in Germany (see Barak 2012, 175–210), but spread into EU Member States' national legal systems through the two European Courts, seated in Strasbourg and Luxembourg. This also applies in Canada, and more recently in Australia, New Zealand, South Africa and many other constitutional fields. For a comprehensive analysis of national and international experiences with respect to the principle of proportionality, see Stone Sweet and Mathews (2008, 73).

7 See, in particular, Italian Constitutional Court Judgement 1130 (1988).

Even in Italian Constitutional Court case law, connecting the 'reasonableness' control with the 'weighting' technique (widely used within American and German constitutional justice systems), involves an approach according to which fundamental rights can never be affirmed in absolute terms. This is, in fact, where the requirement to use this interpretive and argumentative technique derives from. It is, therefore, an interpretative choice that is in line with the plurality of values upon which the Italian constitution stands[8] If it were not so, "one right would become a 'tyrant' in relation to other constitutionally recognized and protected legal interests which, taken together, form expressions of human dignity".[9] According to the Constitutional Court, in order to preserve the "essential core" of fundamental rights, one must assess the balance via reasonableness and proportionality.

However, since the weighing technique applies not only between legal interests but also between opposing principles, the problem of individualization of 'the highest principles'[10] emerges. This individualization cannot be merely 'technical' insofar as its selection cannot be carried out without tracing it back to constitutional values.

While the importance of the interpretative criteria above cannot be underestimated, Barbera questions if reasonableness is possible when weighing rights and principles, without relying on the meaning of 'rational' in a specific culture and in a given material order.[11] And how can terms like 'freedom or dignity of the person' (*et similia*) be used, regardless of the same material order?

These changes in the material order demonstrate the dual nature of the relation between dignity and rights. The very value of human dignity,[12] established in the constitutions of the post–World War II period, runs the

---

8 On this point, see, among others: (Bin 2002; Cartabia 2013).

9 This is what the Italian Constitutional Court, in the famous judgement 85 of 2013, confirmed through the interpretive and argumentative technique of weighting two conflicting rights: on the one hand, the right to health and the environment, and on the other hand, the right to work and to exercise economic activities (Italian Constitutional Court, Judgement 85 of 2013).

10 According to the court, both explicitly and implicitly enshrined principles are considered 'supreme', whether absolute limits to the power of constitutional review are expressly mentioned in the constitution, or "those, though not expressly mentioned [. . .] are part of the essence of the supreme values upon which the Italian Constitution is founded" (Judgement 1146 of 29 December 1988).

11 See Barbera (2015, 269–270).

12 Theories concerning this subject are numerous and quite relevant, even for Italian constitutional scholars. See Ridola (2006), Di Ciommo (2010), Ferrari (2011), Mezzetti 2013, and Ruggeri (2014).

risk of incurring the same generality and ambiguity as the Kelsenian *Grund-norm*.[13] To avoid a such risk, it is vital to clarify how human dignity, as the epitome of the fundamental principles of freedom and equality, assumes an external support function of the legal order and a legitimate source of its validity *supremitas*. Dignity "raises the balance criterion between values, without being susceptible to being reduced itself by such weighting. As a matter of fact, dignity is not an effect of weighing, but the weighting itself" (Silvestri 2009, 87).

The problem of the constitutional interpreter originates from the fact that currently, when social conflict is inevitable, the balancing weights and measures change, depending on the meaning we proffer to social relations and to one's own dignity. This makes the interpreter's task, establishing a balance between interests and principles, according to recognizable and creative criteria, a supremely challenging one. Hence, interpretation moves at a slow, cautious pace, taking baby steps and accommodating certain restrictions, such as the margin of discretion, legal certainty and the certainty of rights (i.e. guarantees of fundamental rights).

Judges who, in carrying out their duties, put their social role and judicial autonomy into play, are extremely aware of the responsibility on their shoulders. Indeed, judicial activity is directed towards the satisfaction of vital (material and ideal) needs, to the protection of fundamental rights and to respect for human dignity. As such, it is not immediately clear how the judge's role poses the risk of *juristocracy*. Could it be that this non-existent threat appears as the result of a real vacuum, or weakness, in the political sphere?

In some cases, the creative responsibility of the judge is undoubtedly enlarged when dealing with such a "real" gap.

The Englaro case is a landmark case in Italy.[14] The Italian Court of Cassation judgement of 4 October 2007 ruled that, in the case of a legal gap, the dispute must be resolved by directly applying the Italian constitution. Was it a real legal gap, though?[15] Or was it perhaps a discretionary move on the part of the interpreter to 'create' a surmountable gap, only via direct application of the constitution? Or could it be, perhaps, that the Italian Supreme Court carried out a constitutionality review

---

13 On this point, see, among others Häberle (2000) and Silvestri (2009, 85).
14 This was the case of Eluana Englaro: her father, given her "permanent vegetative state" requested that the court suspend means of artificial nutrition and hydration.
15 According to the Civil Court of Lecco – as ruled in judgement of 2 March 1999 – there was no legal gap, qualifying the facts at hand as part of Article 579 of the Penal Code (translator's note: this provision establishes the voluntary homicide offence).

upon certain rules that, despite being enshrined in Italian law, were flying in the face of the constitution?[16]

The Englaro case is an obvious consequence of the lack of regulation by State legislature on the issue of a living will – a concrete example of judges filling gaps generated by political players. When the legislator does not intervene, it must be the interpreter (supreme courts and constitutional courts) who enforces a 'new right', especially one which is recognized as inviolable. However, the Italian constitutional case law has adopted a theory in which Article 2 of the constitution must be interpreted as a *numerus apertus* ('open-ended') clause (Barbera 1975), in order to recognize new constitutional rights that arise from social development and are not expressly set out in the constitutional text. For instance, the Italian Constitutional Court, when recognizing the social right to housing as an inviolable right[17] for both citizens and foreigners, altered the meaning of 'inviolability'. It is no longer a merely negative guarantee against abuses and/or intrusions into a person's private life on the part of the State, but it has become a part of the social State obligations and commitments for the effective oversight of fundamental rights, which revolve around the free development of personality.

Similarly, the European Court of Human Rights has adopted an interpretive method in accordance with the object and scope of the European Convention on Human Rights (ECHR), which goes beyond the text itself (Matscher 2009, 903). Thus, thanks to the ECHR case law, a qualitative extension of the protected rights has been established – an extension also favoured by national Constitutional Courts. In this regard, the Italian Constitutional Court has established that a State or regional law that contradicts the provisions of the ECHR – the rules on the implementation of the Convention, in particular – goes against Article 117.1 of the Italian Constitution (Judgements 348 and 349/2007).

All these judicial actions are sufficient to exemplify the importance of the role of the interpreter and, above all, the creative activity of the judge, within the framework of legal orders, as opposed to *common law* jurisdictions.

Similarly the legislator, from the outset, also needs to strike a balance between constitutionally protected principles, rules and interests. However, the legislative intervention risks the abandonment of constitutional principles when the ideological stance of the majority is against them. In fact, if this were to happen, constitutional court judges should act more frequently as a 'corrective' body, and constitutional guarantee mechanism, to ensure adherence and respect for the constitution is maintained, particularly

16 See Articles 2, 13 and 22 of the Italian Constitution.
17 See Italian Constitutional Court Judgement 404/1988.

with regards to the political power. This judicial activity acquires a greater importance when settling potential conflicts that may arise between the democratic expression of the popular will, (with its potential *dictatorship of the majority*), and the protection of the rights of individuals, groups and minorities, through the interpretation of constitutional principles (as an expression of values shared by a historically individualistic society).

Moreover, the positivist conception of the law, especially in its nineteenth century adaptation, has led to an (effective) primacy of the executive over the legislator in Europe, and of the latter over the judiciary, contrary to the nature of a democratic state based on the rule of law, where the constitution prevails. The essence of a democratic political system therefore depends on public authorities' respect for the constitution.

In fact, thanks to the supremacy of the constitution over political powers, on the one hand, and the superior value of human dignity on the other, fundamental rights and democracy in both post-war pluralist democracies became essential. This strong connection between fundamental rights and democracy initiated a movement that opted for a critical re-reading of legal positivism theories, as well as an evaluation of the notion of democracy from an axiological perspective. On the one hand, we have a strictly formal definition of democracy that identifies itself only with regards to respect for legal forms and procedures suitable to guarantee the will of the people, in particular, the will of the majority (Ferrajoli 2009, 1). On the other hand, we are looking at a formal, procedural idea of the constitution and, ultimately, of the law as no longer sufficient. Consequently, it would be preferable to resurrect the old category of equity as a constitutive legal rule, abandoning the concept of law according to which rules are mainly attributable to the coercive orders of the political sovereign. Law as equity implies a balance that must constantly review, from a modern perspective, the principle of separation of powers.

That is precisely why confrontation over legitimacy between constitutional bodies makes little sense within constitutional democracies. A separation of powers and a system of mutual checks and balances, even including conflicts with respect to constitutional legality, are important. Conflict, of course, is inevitable and, within the limits of constitutional rules and principles, might even prove healthy: this is where social and institutional dissent takes shape. Constitutions are based on (unanimous or, at least, almost unanimous) *consensus*[18] and, in a symmetrical way, the basis of the

---

18 *Free and conscientious consensus* should be the basis of each norm, not only within national, but also supranational and international law.

democratic method lies in dissent, which must be expressed by both society and institutional apparatus.

In some jurisdictions, for example, the *dissenting opinion* of one or more judges against the majority decision is quite expected. In the United States, Supreme Court rulings are not necessarily unanimous: the names of those who, despite agreeing with the final ruling, dissent from their reasoning (*concurring opinion*) as well as those who disagree with the final decision (*dissenting opinion*) are referenced in the judgement itself. Likewise, Germany and Spain also provide for individual (concurring or dissenting) opinions, while proposals have been made to introduce this in Italy, for example.[19] Why is the *dissenting opinion* so important? Its main function is to highlight the faults and defects of the majority view, opening the door to possible and subsequent corrections and adjustments of their interpretation. The *dissenting opinion* is a form of constructive criticism, potentially influencing the evolution of the jurisprudence and exercising a decisive influence on legislative activity. Proof of the latter is the dissenting opinion of US Supreme Court justices Curtis and McLean in the *Dred Scott v Sanford* case, 60 US 393 of 1857, on slavery.

In this regard, the distance between public debate and public arguments leading to parliamentary decisions on the one hand, and real, unpublicized in-chamber arguments on the other hand, narrows (all of which is clearly seen in those systems which do not provide for *dissenting opinions*). In this way, the protection of fundamental rights is removed: beginning with freedom of expression and the press of the majority of the elected, and aided by the internal majority of a Court.

In the United States, Supreme Court justices, through an individual opinion, defend the written and timeless constitution, hence guaranteeing the rigidity of its principles. Even in times of greater uncertainty, they safeguard it from legalistic inclusions, removing it from the dominant perspective of a particular generation. Dissenting opinions preserve principles discarded today for the jurists of tomorrow; they keep the values and democratic ideals underlying constitutional principles themselves alive.

The US experience confirms that the dangers to democracy come not from 'governing judges' or the expansion of the law, but from an overriding tendency towards economic primacy, stimulated whenever there is little or no citizen participation in public and political life. For this reason, the implementation of the constitution and the interpretation of

---

19 See: (Mortati 1964; Anzon 1995; Panizza 1998; Cassese 2009; Asprella 2012).

its principles, beginning with that of equality, involves not only all the State's powers, but also its citizens and social groups. It is exactly this involvement which allows constitutional principles to evolve, and stand the test of time.

3.2 Evolutionary interpretation of the equality principle

In a democratic society, the clash between equality and freedom involves a categorical error: the application of freedom without equality and founded on privilege (*unequal liberty*) through a system of norms can only render an oligarchy at the mercy of the strongest groups. On the contrary, the application of "egalitarian freedom", understood as a synonym of social justice, pursues "*democratic* and truly universal aspirations of *merit*" (Della Volpe 1957, 42). Such aspirations are possible if, in counterbalancing the main factors of inequality, the objective is to offer everyone the same opportunities to compete on the basis of merit. It is only from this perspective of equal social freedom that individual capacities can reflect an 'effective' freedom of choice between different alternatives and, at the same time, not only constitute a result of social promotion of equal opportunities and one's own individual capacities[20] but also require the ability to invest in education, training and knowledge in order to produce and improve human capital (Becker 1964).

The Italian Constitutional Court, considering the principle of substantial equality, calls into question the idea that the 'abstract individual' can develop his or her preferences, without taking into account the socio-economic context in which he or she acts. For this reason, social rights are crucial, since they have a very specific, instrumental value: contributing to the removal of economic and social obstacles that impede the full development of the individual, as well as the effective participation of all workers in the political, social and social organization of the nation (Article 3. 2 of the Italian Constitution).

In applying these fundamental principles, the law can – and *must* – react to involuntary inequalities, stemming from or against the will of the person suffering them. An example of such is the disparity between men and women.

Substantial equality is therefore useful in offering 'everyone' the same opportunities, especially through policies and standards that benefit

---

20 On this point, see, among others Rawls (1982), Sen (2001), Dworkin (2002), Carter (2005), De Caro (2009) and Savater (2003).

vulnerable groups and disadvantaged minorities. For example, the constitution of India provides for "positive discrimination" (Article 15): positive actions in favour of certain categories such as women, children, disadvantaged groups of citizens from a view socio-educational point of view, and vulnerable castes and recognized tribal communities (whether by the constitution or by other secondary legislation).

3.3 *Homo oeconomicus* in a liquid society

A major obstacle in the way of promotion of opportunities may derive from the inability of States and international organizations to account for the primacy of the economy over politics or economic freedoms over social rights, respectively. The accelerating process of economic globalization accentuates the tendency to think of (political) economy as a kind of *sovereign science* upon which politics, the law, the State and the very concept of 'constitution' automatically depend. This 'mechanical' link, however, constitutes a misunderstanding that hinders analysis of mutually affected relations between the law, economics and politics. In these circumstances, both modern, anti-ideological Marxist thought and the 'meagreness' of Marx's State theory resurface.[21]

One problem undoubtedly remains. Economic institutions, regardless of the human subsistence (Polany 1983) may condition, and even prevail, over other stakeholders. Institutions tend, as a result of self-regulation (which is not only efficient but also effective, since it is often not subject to restriction), to transform consensus into a simple approval, citizens into mere consumers and work into merchandise; and where political institutions and social control is at its weakest, they tend to transform the earth and the environment into a contaminating waste disposal site. Even in contexts where there is little of this destruction in evidence, *homo oeconomicus* still suffers deep discomfort in a liquid society: seeking to unite the various aspects of life in a dimension in which the *social individual* dominates.

---

21 Francesco Salvatore Merlino harshly critiques "economic fatalism" of the "Marxists". The author, who was linked, albeit in an original form, to a branch of legal socialism, rejected proletariat dictatorship and any form of despotism, and in particular emphasized the solid link between exasperated Marxist economism and the dictatorship of the proletariat. Though State history is implicitly linked to that of the economic system, this does not, according to Merlino, prevent them from being two related but wholly different phenomena. For this reason, Merlino criticizes what he calls the "impermanence" of Marx and Engels' State theory. For more on Merlino's Legal Socialist Theory, see: (Galizia 1977, 531–634).

This uneasiness only increases as a result of global economic and financial crises, which in many Member States of the European Union have truly tested the maintenance of social rights[22] (the right to work, the right to health, the right to an education, and so on). Gross Domestic Product (GDP) is not enough to tackle these growing inequalities. Only the rich are concerned about the GDP, because economic growth measured through this indicator brings together maximum benefits for that particular group. For this reason, it is appropriate to change the indicators of economic growth and, above all, European *welfare*.

A critical reflection on the relations between politics and the economy is undoubtedly advisable, although it is difficult to imagine a return to primitive forms of protectionism in Europe. Hence, it would seem that an exclusively state approach to economic and social life, understood as a useful measure to counter economic globalization and protect fundamental rights, should be enough.[23]

3.4 The Islamic veil and rational fundamentalism

The issue of equality is much more complex today, since we are currently confronted with societies that have increasingly multicultural connotations. For this reason, a substantial equality framework cannot look only to traditional economic–social divisions. The problem of equality and the protection of fundamental rights have repercussions over many issues, which are not only closely linked, but can also be redirected to a substantive issue that involves a global legal consideration, beyond fortress towns. It is a question of redefining the links between individuals, community and the State – through a dynamic, focused approach to legal research. This means focusing inside and outside our borders, and looking not only at legal statements, but at real problems and people. It means carrying out research which, in the face of increasing globalization and multiculturalism, encourages the respect and integration of different cultures, even those cultures which do not place *homo oeconomicus* at the heart of social action.

For example, a lawyer, when facing new emerging problems in multicultural societies, must relativize the Christian cultural component that lies behind legal categories, in order to try and "develop a model of legal

22 See Jimena (2014, 13), Carney et al. (2014, 312–332), Rodrigues (2015), Maestri (2014), Aravantinou Leonidi (2015) and Ruiz-Rico Ruiz (2015).
23 In the context of the debate on the future of the European Union, this subject has been much discussed. Against the return of intergovernmental national forces and in favour of completing the European integration process, see J. Habermas, Italian edition 2013.

subjectivity, and hence, of legal semantics that is equidistant from both Christian and *other* religions" (Ricca 2008, 131).

In some cases, governments, legislators and courts themselves do not support, and at times hinder, social integration and cultural protection of immigrants by violating the most fundamental rights of the person – in particular, of women.

In October 1989, as the Berlin Wall was falling in Germany, another wall was being built in France, on behalf of the principle of State secularism: a Muslim student who did not want to remove her Islamic veil, as demanded by school authorities and teachers, was denied access to the classroom. This particular veil was not the kind that covers the entire face, but the headscarf (the *chador*). This garment did not obstruct normal facial recognition, nor did it impede relations between individuals. These facts focused the case purely on the legality of the presence of religious symbols in French schools. According to the French supreme administrative court, the *Conseil d'Etat* failed to convincingly solve the problem and reduce tensions, arguing that when this event occurred, only 200 Muslim students, out of the 300,000 who were in school, wore a veil (although following this incident, its use spread quickly).

In France, two acts have been successively adopted regarding these issues: the first in 2004,[24] which prohibited, in primary and secondary schools, the use of symbols or attire that showed membership of a particular religion, and the second, in 2010[25] (in force since 11 April 2011), which established an absolute ban on the use of the veil if it partially or completely covered the face. The 2004 act was seen as the 'anti-veil Act' by the Muslim community (despite referring to all religious groups), perceived to have been created out of a secularism that divides rather than unites;[26] a 'militant secularism' (*laïcité de combat*) or as a repudiating and restricting secularism, rather than something which reflected the original idea of a pacifying, respectful secularism with positive neutrality. This act, which spectacularly failed to facilitate integration and social cohesion, seemed to respond to Islamic fundamentalism with its own form of rational fundamentalism.

In the 2010 act the Strasbourg Court[27] upheld that this act did not constitute a violation of the ECHR, in general, nor the right to respect for

---

24 Act 2004–228, of 15 March 2004, in application of the principle of secularism, on the use of signs or attire that manifest religious belonging in public schools, colleges and schools.
25 Act 2010–1192, of 11 October 2010, prohibiting concealment of the face in public spaces.
26 A secularity that unites "leads to the understanding of differences, without any option being imposed on others from a higher position" (Prisco 2009, 15; Modood 2009, 71–76).
27 Judgement of 1 July 2014, *S.A.S. v Francia* (43835/11).

private and family life, freedom of thought, conscience and religion and, most specifically, the right not to suffer any kind of discrimination. However, the legislation and especially the 2004 act, have come under heavy fire by international organizations fighting for human rights protection, such as Amnesty International.[28] Such organizations argued that the legislation denied Muslim women their right to manifest their religious beliefs and not be discriminated against for them.

Compared to France, German constitutional case law has shown a very different approach to the use of the veil, based on the principle of open and broad (*offene und übergreifende*) neutrality and on the daily exercise of tolerance as a way to enable integration.[29] In the judgement of March 2015, the German Federal Constitutional Court issued a decision concerning a complaint lodged by two female teachers who had been convicted by the labour court under *Länder* after refusing to remove their veil during class time. The German Constitutional Court specifically used the principle of "positive" secularity, with a rationale emphasizing a "case by case" analysis of situations in which a religious symbol can compromise the full guarantee of rights in a "secular" State.

The ratio decidendi, or the rationale for the decision of the German Federal Constitutional Court, is based on the principle that, in order to justify a ban, "it is not enough that the manifestation of religious convictions constitutes an abstract danger, but must harm the peace in school or the duty of neutrality on behalf of the State" (D'Amico 2015, 31). The Court also emphasized that regional law violates the constitutional prohibition of discrimination on religious grounds (Article 3.3 and 33.3 of the BL), by not creating a similar ban for Christian symbols. There is no doubt that the decision of Constitutional Court judges depends on the interpretation and evaluation of the socio-historical context, in which public schools may be of an 'inter-denominational' nature, reflecting a plural and multicultural society.

3.5 The application of the equality principle to foreigners

As outlined earlier, the debate on multicultural societies requires an interpretation of constitutional principles, so as to promote social cohesion through the application of equality in the field of the fundamental rights of foreigners.

28 See 2012 Amnesty International report: *Choice and prejudice. Discrimination against Muslims in Europe.*
29 Constitutional Court of the Federal Republic of Germany (BVerfG) Judgement of 24 September 2003, 2 BvR 1436/0.

When the Italian Constitution was drafted, the problem of migration flows in Italy was only about emigration: at that time it was difficult to predict that a war-torn country would become the destination for a massive influx of irregular immigrants. It is not surprising that Article 35.3 of the Italian Constitution emphasizes the recognition of "the freedom to emigrate, safeguarding obligations established by law in the public interest, and protects Italian labour abroad".

The provision contained in this article as a whole seems to leave few doubts about its *ratione personae*: Italians living abroad, as well as those not belonging to the Republic. However, change in migration flows necessitates new interpretations, especially as the protection foreseen refers to emigration in general, even for foreigners in Italy. The wording itself establishes the freedom to emigrate without specifying that such freedom is only recognized for Italian citizens. Similarly, and in order to confirm this interpretation, reference should be made to the preparatory work in the drafting of the constitution, whereby the need for gradual elimination of international controls and obligations with respect to free movement of workers emerges clearly, in order to fight against demographic isolation and bans on immigration so burdensome for Italian workers.[30]

The supporters in favour of this interpretation seek to find a constitutional foundation of a limited right to immigration, for labour-related reasons.

Despite this, the most relevant aspect is not so much the existence of a true right to immigration or lack thereof, but rather the fact that, due to unstoppable migratory flows, fundamental rights of the foreigner, in accordance with the fundamental principles of the constitutional order, are necessary. This stems from the principle of equality, taking into account that Article 2 of the Italian Constitution must be considered as an "open-ended provision": a norm that can cover all "the new demands of freedom voiced by social awareness" (Barbera 1975, 50).

According to the case law of the Italian Constitutional Court, among others,[31] there can be no doubt that the dignity of the person and the

---

30 See Falzone et al. (1976, 128).

31 The Spanish Constitutional Court, for example, has affirmed on numerous occasions that some fundamental rights affect the person by merely being such, regardless of citizenship (Judgement 242/1994, 91/2000, 236/2007 and 259/2007). For an in-depth study of the Spanish Constitutional Court case law, see a recent essay by Pérez Sola (2015, 217).

principle of equality also affect foreigners,[32] even if the constitutional provision only makes reference to "citizens" (Article 3, Italian Constitution). Renowned academics have rebutted this conclusion (Pace 2003, 315), since Italian Constitutional Court judgement 120/1967, Article 3 of the Constitution was interpreted beyond its literal wording. Thus, it has applied the principle of equality in an extensive way, to include the sphere of the fundamental rights of the foreigner. In 1979, the Constitutional Court emphasized that "textual reference to Article 3.1. citizens does not preclude [. . .] that equality before the law is also guaranteed for foreigners when it comes to ensuring the protection of a person's inviolable rights".[33]

However, even into the 1990s, the Constitutional Court judge allowed the legislative to establish "reasonable" differences in relation to citizenship.[34] Only in Constitutional Court Judgement 198/2000 was it finally established that the foreigner, regardless of his or her regular or "irregular" status, should enjoy all fundamental rights.[35]

This gradual recognition of fundamental rights towards foreigners did not provoke any socio-political tensions, as the phenomenon of migration in Italy until the 1980s was not significant. In the past, much more attention was paid to the freedom to emigrate and to the protection of Italian workers abroad, in accordance with the provisions of the Italian Constitution (Article 35, last paragraph).

However, if the current growth of the migratory phenomenon is not adequately addressed at both national and European levels, political forces may begin to adopt a language regarding the fundamental rights of foreigners which is in accordance with criteria related to nationality, or even denial of rights. The 2014 elections to the European Parliament have confirmed the success of these political parties and movements, whose presence has been strengthened in countries such as France and the United Kingdom.

In opposition is the certainty of rights extending to social and political rights for foreigners with regular residence. Social rights, by their very nature,[36] are

---

32 However, it should be noted that Article 10.2 of the Italian Constitution, by providing for the legal regulation of the legal status of foreigners in accordance with international norms and treaties, has exceeded Article 16 of the Italian Civil Code (general legal provisions), according to which the foreigner may enjoy the same rights as the citizen under conditions of reciprocity. This has led to the opening up of international human rights law and the consequent recognition of a fundamental rights statute to every individual for the simple fact of being human.

33 See Constitutional Court Judgement 54/1979.

34 See Constitutional Court judgements 244/1994 and 62/1994.

35 See Constitutional Court Judgement 252/2001 concerning the right to health.

36 Indeed, the theory of the highest exclusive cost of social rights is erroneous. In this regard, see Jimena Quesada (2016).

"costly rights",[37] which together with political rights, favour integration and social cohesion. Likewise, in the face of weak social rights that increase an intentionally amplified 'perception' of fear, public opinion tends to react to the migration phenomenon by defending a xenophobic conception of citizenship and supporting policies that build walls of rules set, primarily, to defend security and public order. Italy in recent years has seen all of this happen.

In some cases, these are conspicuously unconstitutional rules – for example, those sanctioning a *status* and not a material conduct, which implies an aggravating circumstance in the determination of the penalty for only certain people (stateless and non-European citizens). These rules violate not only the principle of equality, but also the provisions of Article 25. 2 of the Italian Constitution, which establishes the factual basis of criminal responsibility, clearly indicating that a person must be punished for his or her conduct and not for his or her personal qualities.[38] In this case, the rules contrast with a "liberally inspired criminal notion [that] must pay attention to the need to weigh repressive efficiency with respect to the individual's guarantees of rights" (Fiandaca and Musco 2002, 21).

It seems highly unreasonable to think that, in order to deal with the phenomenon of immigration, identifying it as a mere public security issue (a presumption of danger with respect to an 'irregular' situation) can be seen as compatible with the Italian constitutional order. The Constitutional Court has already established that "the lack of proper documentation that allows remaining on national territory . . . cannot be a factor [. . .] of social danger".[39] Despite this, the inclusion of a crime of illegal immigration could not be prevented.[40]

All this is evidence of a direction that goes totally against that of a human rights citizenship taken in the past. Nonetheless it seems that, the italian legislative is showing signs of going against this past trend. Limits and contradictions are still present: even in recent immigration legislation, a reflection of this trend can be deduced from the 'decriminalisation' of illegal immigration.[41]

---

37 This expression has been used in Italy – even in reference to political rights – by Pace (2009) and also by D'Atena (2012, 972). It was later brought back by Pace (2010) and Stancati (2010, 103). Nevertheless, this notion can be seen in earlier works, such as Holmes, and Sunstein (1999), Bin (2000).

38 See Constitutional Court Judgement 249/2010.

39 See Constitutional Court Judgement 78/2007.

40 Act of 15 July 2009: Provisions on public safety (*Gazzetta Ufficiale* number 170, 24 July 2009).

41 Act 67/2014.

3.6 The constitutional principle on the value of labour and participation as fundamental social rights extended to Italian and foreign workers

The immigration phenomenon is not marginal at all if we look at it from a numerical,[42] cultural and legal standpoint. From a legal perspective, the most problematic aspect is whether to consider a re-reading of the constitution and its dynamic interpretation in order to draft new norms.

First, it is important to analyse a specific aspect: as deduced both from the "social groups" reference found in the Italian Constitution and a systematic reading of its fundamental principles – there is no room for a solely 'negative' approach to fundamental rights.

As explained earlier, the Italian Constitution rejects abstract individualism and gives value to community personalism. It places the 'person' in his or her particular social action and living conditions. It gives value to the need of understanding the 'person' via the rights possessed.[43] The Italian Constitution marks the link between freedom and substantial equality, setting up an important connection between the recognition of rights and the necessary removal of all economic and social conditions of inequality, which prevents both the full development of the person, and "the effective participation of all workers in the political, economic and social organisation of the country" (Article 3, Italian Constitution).

Thus, the notion of participation is linked to the principle of work as a founding element of the Italian Republic, understood "in all its forms and applications" (Article 35.1) as a factor of unity and inclusion. In fact, according to the Italian Constitution, work is a means that contributes to the development of personality and to the material and spiritual progress of society. Work, here, comes from a different perspective than that of the leading economic ideology, which reduces the social dimension of work to the point of turning productive individualism into myth. This is particularly evident when, for example, maximizing business profit is the lone objective, and other values are ignored.

---

42 Italy, as of 1 January 2014, has 4,922,085 foreign residents, 18.1% of the current population (60,782,668 inhabitants). The 2014 Statistical Immigration Dossier, prepared by IDOS on behalf of the National Anti-Racial Discrimination Office (UNAR), estimates, however, that on that date, legal residents in Italian territory included approximately 5,364,000 foreigners, after adding the quota of the foreign population that "despite being legally resident, have not (still) been registered in the Registry Office". For a better idea of the procedure and estimates, see UNAR (2014, 113–114). Sure enough, there is an increasing presence of foreigners, both in absolute and relative terms, but parallel in comparison with the increase in other EU Member States.

43 There is noted disagreement about the notion of 'person', although the fact that the person is entitled to rights in not in question.

Hence, the value of work can be explained in its relation to participation as a constitutional principle, and the fact that more than just the political right of the citizen-voter, it is rather a right of a person, either as an individual, or group where personality is developed, (Article 2, Italian Constitution). Additionally, it is precisely through the relationship between constitutional freedoms and Article 2[44] that, in the past, readings of the Constitution were made that were aimed at extending civil and political rights to foreigners, even when the literal nature of the provisions (notably, freedom of assembly of Article 17 and freedom of association in Article 18) refers to "citizens".[45]

Nevertheless, first and foremost, the connection between participation and the constitutional principle of work must be carefully analyzed. This link is a gateway through which the right to participation can be recognized to all workers, including foreigners, by highlighting it as the right to *social citizenship*.

3.7 Towards a fundamental rights citizenship

Social citizenship is not equivalent to legal citizenship *sensu stricto*, since the latter is configured, as in international law, as the right of the individual to a nationality,[46] as part of a human rights citizenship.

Yet as more of us are increasingly moving from one country to another, it is simply illogical that nationality is determined by a simple blood link or by place of birth, *ius sanguinis* or *ius soli*, respectively, and that these are the sole necessary conditions for the enjoyment of rights. More than a general right to nationality, it would be more appropriate to establish the right to a nationality, to be conferred not by a State itself, in the absence of effective ties with it, but by the State in which the individual has chosen to settle and develop their activities (Panella 2012). This is a very desirable approach, for it radically alters the relationship between the individual and the State. It

---

44 On this point, see, among others: Barile (1966), Pace (1977), Borrello (1989) and Prisco (1991).

45 However, both Article 11 of the ECHR and Article 20 of the Universal Declaration of Human Rights recognize that everyone has the right to freedom of peaceful assembly and freedom of association.

46 The individual right to a nationality is provided for in the 1969 American Convention on Human Rights, which substantially reproduces Article 15 of the Universal Declaration of Human Rights. The Inter-American Court of Human Rights, which ruled on this issue in its judgement of 8 September 2005 in the *Yean and Bosico v Dominican Republic* case, defined the right to a nationality as a "fundamental right of the human person". At the European level, there is the European Convention on Nationality, which came into force in 2000, as well as the Council of Europe Convention on the Avoidance of Statelessness in Relation to State Succession, in force since May 2009.

becomes even more powerful if a truly supranational European *ius soli*: the right to European homeland is adopted (Papisca 2013, 27).

The Italian Constitutional Court has already accepted the effective nationality criterion in Judgement 227 of 24 June 2010, in which the citizenship requirement linked to nationality is surmounted by a substantial residence requirement (Finck 2015, 78–98), or in other words, the effective link of an individual with a Member State of the European Union.[47] However, in this case, a reference is made to the European public space extending economic, cultural, civil and social rights to all individuals, regardless of the link to any Member State of the European Union. In short, this issue affects European citizens.

The issue of an open, inclusive citizenship also affects long-term foreign residents in the European Union. To this purpose, the Tampere European Council of 15 and 16 October 1999 recommended that Member States should reach an agreement regarding the recognition of EU citizenship and the rights derived from them to third-country nationals who had been granted long-term legal residence in any EU Member State. Despite this suggestion, later confirmed in the Stockholm Program for the period 2010–2014, no further action has yet been taken.

On the contrary, the Italian Constitution offers more than one argument in favour of the idea of a citizenship exclusively linked to a stable residence in the national territory by recognizing the right of asylum to foreigners, who, in their home country, are denied the "actual exercise of the democratic freedoms" (Article 10, Italian Constitution) that are guaranteed by the Italian legal order.

Another argument in favour of inclusive citizenship can be found within the automatic and "permanent" (Perassi 1950) adaptation of the Italian legal system to generally recognized rules of international law (see Article 10, 1 of the Italian Constitution), confirmed by the constitutional amendment of Article 117, which introduced the obligation to respect conventional and customary international law. This open acceptance of international values is now considered standard in fundamental Italian constitutional principles. Accordingly, legislative regulation of a foreigner's legal situation must also conform to international norms and treaties (Article 10.2), which prevail over the reciprocity requirement provided in Article 16 of the Civil Code, according to which "a foreigner may

---

47 The unconstitutionality of Article 8 of Act 69 of 2005, implementing the Framework Decision concerning the European arrest warrant, which allowed the execution of the arrest warrant to be refused if they were Italian citizens, was concluded. Following the court's decision, this possibility has also been extended to community citizens residing in Italy.

enjoy the rights attributed to citizens on the basis of reciprocity". This last provision, following the entry into force of the republican constitution, is understood to be implicitly repealed.

Taking into account principles, norms and constitutional case law as well as international human rights law, widely introduced in the Italian legal order, fundamental rights are gradually being extended to all individuals. In addition, the substantial residence requirement, the effective link with a country, together with the principle of the full participation of all workers in a country's political, economic and social organizational arena, can be the basis for the recognition of full citizenship.

In addition to granting social rights to foreigners who regularly reside for two years in Italy or in an EU Member State and who have contributed to public expenditure according to their capacities, both the right to vote in municipal elections and, two years later, the right to legal citizenship *stricto sensu*, should also be recognized. If this is necessary for first-generation adult immigrants, then greater protection should be given to minors. Hence, a new way of obtaining Italian nationality by birth (through *ius soli*) and another new procedure for acquiring nationality after a period of schooling (called *ius culturae*)[48] should be envisaged.

The adoption of new legislation on nationality can be a great step towards the achievement of this open and inclusive citizenship.

3.8 From a universal rights rhetoric towards an intercultural European citizenship

The evolutionary interpretation of constitutional principles works by defining fundamental rights content in accordance with their socio-cultural context, and thus, going beyond the generic universality of human rights rhetoric.

Human rights require temporary, spatial and organizational recognition, as well as well thought out rules that aim at their effective protection. Unfortunately, Australia's proposal, submitted to the Human Rights Commission

---

48 On 13 October 2015, the assembly of the Italian Chamber of Deputies adopted and transferred a unified text on citizenship that introduces the aforementioned innovations to the Senate. The text also provides for a transitional regime. Those who have met the requirements to obtain nationality by means of *iure culturae* before the entry into force of the legislation and who have already reached 20 years of age (the limit provided by law for the declaration on acquiring nationality), can request it within 12 months after its entry into force, provided they have resided in Italy for at least five years.

in 1948, regarding the creation of an international court of human rights[49] was never adopted. It was only following the Cold War and the atrocities in Yugoslavia and Rwanda that the UN Security Council established two *ad hoc* tribunals (in 1993 and 1994, respectively).The Rwandan experience and the refusal of some States to recognize violence as genocide made fundamental human rights protection (Katzenstein 2014, 191)[50] seem illusory.

It was therefore necessary to create a strong and independent tribunal, the International Criminal Court (ICC) to deter future atrocities and validate human rights systems. This court's jurisdiction covers crimes committed in the territory of a State Party or by a citizen of a State Party, including crimes committed in a State Party by a citizen who does not belong to a State Party.

However, despite the fact that the ICC statute came into force on 1 July 2002, after ratification by the sixtieth State, it is well known that neither the United States, Russia nor China, (three of the five UN Security Council Member States), have acceded to it.

The protection of human rights, even today, is essentially guaranteed by the constitutional systems of democratic States and by regional human rights protection systems (ECHR, European Union, American Convention, etc.).[51] These legal systems act as a public space for fundamental rights and freedoms, open to the recognition of more than national or purely identity citizenship. In this way, a new 'righteous' relationship between global and local approaches ('glocalism') is created – a relationship that does not return to the past and to closed borders, without cultural boundaries, and which, thanks to the Internet, have been slowly disappearing.

'Glocalism' is useful insofar as it contributes to the breaking down of ideologies (*de-ideologize*) and embedding of human rights, enshrining them in the legal order through principles, norms, procedures and guarantees. Just as with the individual person, neither the law nor rights can be removed from its socio-cultural and historical context.

In this way, a non-static but procedural notion about culture and human rights cultures is made possible by promoting the recognition of these rights through intercultural dialogue and the search for common values and principles. It is a cultural concept at the root of the rediscovery of legal pluralism,

---

49 This proposal was already made by Australia's representative on February 1947 in the UN Economic and Social Council (ECOSOC).

50 For more on the tensions between sovereignty and right to intervene, see Corteu (2012, 33).

51 For an in-depth analysis of the differences and similarities of systems and models for supranational integration in Europe and Latin America, see Sánchez and Jimena (1995), Freire Soares (2011), Carducci (2013, 1–22) and Carducci and De Oliveira (2014).

understood, first of all, as a characteristic of social contexts (Griffiths 1986, 38; Moore 1978, 54–81).

A proof of the virtuous link between global and local frameworks lies in one of the distinctive features of post–World War II constitutional systems: their openness to international law as a way to facilitate international organizations' activity in ensuring peace and justice among nations.[52]

This openness is in harmony with the legal theory that approaches the constitution more as a (historical) 'process' than as an 'act' – punctual in time – and also with the recognition of new rights and their protection both at international, but more especially, national and European levels.

It also corresponds to the primacy of EU law, which is not restricted by any national act or internal rule. Legitimate control of EU rules relating to fundamental rights is exercised by the Court of Justice of the European Union, which has played a very key role in strengthening European citizenship[53] and a *constitutionalism of principles* within Europe. In fact, in the late 1960s, before the Charter of Fundamental Rights of the European Union, and in the absence of a Bill of Rights written in the constituent

52 It is true that not all constitutions have the same degree of openness to human rights treaties, and especially to the ECHR. In the Netherlands, the ECHR has a supra-constitutional value and, in Austria, it holds constitutional value. However, in many other countries, the provisions of the ECHR are below the constitution yet above the rest of ordinary legislation (France, Belgium, Switzerland, Greece, Czech Republic, etc.). Moreover, in some States, the ECHR has similar value to the law (Germany, Finland, Turkey, Hungary and Italy, before the Title V constitutional amendment). On this subject, see Sudre (2009, 194). In the wake of Italy's 2001 constitutional review, the ECHR became superior to ordinary legislation, and the exclusive competence for interpreting its provisions was attributed to the Court of Strasbourg. However, before and after the constitutional amendment procedure, the Italian Constitutional Court insists that direct application of the ECHR is not yet possible. Even so, this approach does not make sense. Firstly, the violation treaty provisions imply condemning or sanctioning the State by the Court of Strasbourg, whose judgements are legally binding. Secondly, given that judges cannot directly override rules in conflict with the ECHR, the hypothesis that the most adequate protection of fundamental rights (for some rights, depending on the cases and particular contexts, for example during cyclical economic-financial crises) is found in the ECHR rather than in national law is excluded. Who, then, has the competence to choose the right substantive rule for the specific case, by adopting an increasing standard of protection of fundamental rights? The answer may lie in the future accession of the European Union to the ECHR and its legal effects. Once in force, it will open the doors of the ambiguous control of "conventionality". With the accession of the European Union to the ECHR, the issue of direct application of the ECHR in Italy has been raised again. See contributions made in Di Blase (2014).
53 'European citizenship' was officially born in 1993, with the entry into force of the first Treaty of the European Union, signed in Maastricht in February 1992. However, its effective date of birth is that of the European Court of Justice ruling of 5 February 1963 with the revolutionary *Van Gend in Loos* case, which recognized citizens of its Member States subjects of rights within the then-called community legal order (Moccia 2013, 12).

treaties, the Court of Justice created an unwritten system of fundamental principles, relating to fundamental rights taken from Member States' common constitutional traditions and from certain international treaties, such as the ECHR. This system of fundamental principles is an exemplary case of *cross-cultural constitutionalism* which, at European level, constitutes the birth of European citizenship.

From the 1960s until the adoption of the Charter of Fundamental Rights of the European Union and its legal recognition in the Lisbon Treaty, a certain degree of progress was made. Yet factors including cyclical economic and financial crises and migration flows caused a deep crisis within European institutions, negatively impacting European integration. The idea of multilevel constitutionalism[54] was found to be no longer adequate in moving the European integration process forward.

The time has passed to abandon the European bureaucratic *governance* and resolve the old issue of the legal nature of the European Union. In order for the European Union to survive, it must be configured as a multicultural federal state whose constituent players can only be European citizens. In other words, it is not the *governance* of differences, but rather the birth of a true, multicultural federal state that values both cultural and institutional pluralism as well as the very concept of European citizenship as intercultural citizenship, that must be established.

References

Anzon, A (ed) (1995) *L'opinione dissenziente*. Giuffrè, Milano.

Aravantinou Leonidi, G (2015) Costituzionalismo e crisi economica. I diritti sociali in Grecia. *Democrazia e sicurezza-Democracy and Security Review* 3.

Asprella, C (2012) *L'opinione dissenziente del giudice*. Aracne, Roma.

Barak, A (2012) *Proportionality*. Cambridge University Press, Cambridge.

Barbera, A (1975) Art. 2. In: Branca, G (ed) *Commentario della Costituzione. Principi fondamentali*. Zanichelli, Bologna.

Barbera, A (2015) Costituzione della Repubblica italiana. *Enciclopedia del diritto*, annali VIII. Giuffrè, Milano.

Barile, P (1951) *La costituzione come norma giuridica*. Sansoni Editore, Firenze.

Barile, P (1966) *Le libertà nella Costituzione*. Cedam, Padova.

Becker, G.S (1964) *Human Capital*. Columbia University Press, New York. Italian edition: (2008) *Il capitale umano*. Laterza, Roma-Bari.

Bin, R (2000) Diritti e fraintendimenti. *Ragion pratica* 14.

---

54 This category was introduced by Ingolf Pernice (1999, 703) so as to represent the broad articulation of the organization of public powers in the European system, on the basis of multiple levels.

Bin, R (2002) Ragionevolezza e divisione dei poteri. In: La Torre, M, Spadaro, A (eds) *La ragionevolezza nel diritto*. Giappichelli, Torino, p. 59 and following.

Borrello, R (1989) Riunione (diritto di). *Enciclopedia del diritto*, annali XL. Giuffrè, Milano.

Carducci, M (2013) Il difficile confronto tra Europa e America latina su diritto giurisprudenziale e tutela multiordinamentale dei diritti fondamentali. *Federalismi.it – Focus Human Rights* 4: 1–22.

Carducci, M, de Oliveira Mazzuoli, V (2014) *Teoria tridimensional das integrações supranacionais*. *Uma análise comparativa dos sistemas e modelos de integração da Europa e América Latina*. Forense-Gen, Rio de Janeiro.

Carney, G.M, Scharf, T, Timonen, V, Conlon, C (2014) 'Blessed are the young, for they shall inherit the national debt': Solidarity Between Generations in the Irish Crisis. *Critical Social Policy* 3: 312–332.

Cartabia, M (2013) Principi di ragionevolezza e proporzionalità nella giurisprudenza costituzionale italiana. *Incontri tra la Corte costituzionale e la Corte costituzionale spagnola e il Tribunale costituzionale portoghese* 3.

Carter, I (2005) *La libertà eguale*. Feltrinelli, Milano.

Cassese, S (2009) Una lezione sulla cosiddetta opinione dissenziente. *Quaderni costituzionali* 4.

Cheli, E (2011) *Stato costituzionale e ragionevolezza*. Napoli, Editoriale Scientifica.

Corteu, O (2012) Droit d'intervention versus souveraineté. Actualité et antécédents d'une tension protéiforme. *Droits* 56: 33 and following.

Crisafulli, V (1952) *La Costituzione e le sue disposizioni di principio*. Giuffrè, Milano.

D'Amico, M (2015) Laicità costituzionale e fondamentalismi tra Italia ed Europa: considerazioni a partire da alcune decisioni giurisprudenziali. *Rivista AIC* 2.

D'Atena, A (ed) (2012) *Studi in onore di Pierfrancesco Grossi*. Giuffrè, Milano.

De Caro, M (2009) *Libero arbitrio. Una introduzione*. Laterza, Roma-Bari.

Della Volpe, G (1957) Il problema della libertà egalitaria nello sviluppo della moderna democrazia: ossia il Rousseau vivo. In: Della Volpe, G (1997) Rousseau e Marx. Editori Riuniti, Roma.

Di Blasé, A (ed) (2014) *Convenzioni sui diritti umani e corti nazionali*. RomaTrE-Press, Roma.

Di Ciommo, M (2010) *Dignità umana e Stato costituzionale*. Passigli Editore, Firenze.

Dogliani, M (1982) *Interpretazioni della Costituzione*. Franco Angeli, Milano.

Dworkin, R (2002) *Virtù sovrana. Teoria dell'uguaglianza*. Feltrinelli, Milano.

Falzone, V, Palermo, F, Cosentino, F (1976) *La Costituzione della Repubblica italiana illustrata con i lavori preparatory*. Mondadori, Milano.

Ferrajoli, L (2009) Democrazia costituzionale e scienza giuridica. *Diritto pubblico* 1: 1 and following.

Ferrari, G.F (2011) *Le libertà. Profili comparatistici*. Giappichelli, Torino.

Fiandaca, G, Musco, E (2002) *Diritto penale. Parte generale*. Bologna, Zanichelli.

Finck, M (2015) Towards an Ever Closer Union Between Residents and Citizens? *European Constitutional Law Review* 11: 78–98.

Frosini, T.E (2009) Gli stranieri tra diritto di voto e cittadinanza. In: Letter, M (ed) *Immigrazione, frontiere sterne e diritti umani. Profili internazionali, europei ed interni. Prefazione di Benedetto Conforti*. Teseo Editore, Rome.

Galizia, M (1977) Il socialismo giuridico di Francesco Saverio Merlino. Dall'anarchismo al socialismo (Alle origini della dottrina socialista dello Stato in Italia). In: *Scritti in onore di Costantino Mortati, 1. Diritto costituzionale generale. Storia costituzionale e politica costituzionale*. Giuffrè, Milano.

Griffiths, J (1986) What Is Legal Pluralism? *Journal of Legal Pluralism and Unofficial Law* 24.

Häberle, P (2000) Constitutional State and Its Reform Requirements. Italian edition: Rossi, S, Politi, F (eds) (2005) *Lo Stato costituzionale*. Istituto della Enciclopedia italiana. Roma.

Habermas, J (2013) Democracy or Capitalism. Italian edition: La miseria capitalistica di una società planetaria integrata economicamente e frantumata in Stati nazionali found. *Nueva Sociedad Journal* 246.

Hirschl, R (2004) *Towards Juristocracy: The Origins and Consequences of the New Constitutionalism*. Harvard University Press, Cambridge.

Holmes, S, Sunstein, C. R (1999) *The Costs of Rights. Why Liberty Depends on Taxes*. W.W. Norton & Co., New York-London. Italian edition: (2000) *Il costo dei diritti*. Il Mulino, Bologna.

Jimena Quesada, L (2014) Introducción: sostenibilidad y efectividad de los derechos sociales, incluso y sobre todo en tiempos de crisis. In: Alfonso Mellado, C.L, Jimena Quesada, L, Salcedo Beltrán, C (eds) *La jurisprudencia del Comité Europeo de Derecho Sociales frente a la crisis económica*. Editorial Bomarzo, Albacete.

Jimena Quesada, L (2016) Immigrati e altre persone vulnerabili: crisi umanitaria e necessaria ottimizzazione degli strumenti che garantiscono i diritti sociali. *Democrazia e sicurezza – Democracy and Security Review* 1.

Katzenstein, S (2014) In the Shadow of Crisis: The Creation of International Courts in the Twentieth Century. *Harvard International Law Journal* 55(1): 193 and following.

Maestri, G (2014) I diritti ai "non cittadini" come fattore di sicurezza? *Democrazia e sicurezza – Democracy and Security Review* 3.

Matscher, F (2009) La Cour européenne des droits de l'homme. Hier, aujourd'hui et demain, au lendemain de son cinquantième anniversaire. *Revue trimestrielle des droits de l'homme* 80.

Maurício Freire Soares, R (2011) Il sistema inter-americano di protezione dei diritti umani. *Democrazia e Sicurezza – Democracy and Security Review* 2.

Mezzetti, L (2013) Storia dei diritti umani. In: Mezzetti, L (ed) *Diritti e doveri*. Giappichelli, Torino.

Moccia, L (2013) Il diritto dei cittadini dell'Unione di avere un governo. *La cittadinanza europea* 1: 5–15.

Modood, T (2009) Moderate Secularism and Multiculturalism. *Politics* 29(1): 71–76.

Modugno, F (1970) *L'invalidità della legge, II, Teoria dell'atto legislativo e oggetto del giudizio costituzionale*. Giuffrè, Milano, p. 6.

72   *Rights and constitutional interpretation*

Moore, S.F (1978) Law and Social Change: The Semi-Autonomous Social Field as an Appropriate Subject of Study. In: *Law as Process: An Anthropological Approach*. Routledge & Kegan Paul, London, pp. 54–81.

Mortati, C (ed) (1964) *Le opinioni dei giudici costituzionali e internazionali*. Giuffrè, Milano.

Pace, A (1977) Art. 17. In: Branca, G (ed) *Commentario della Costituzione italiana*. Zanichelli-Il Foro italiano, Roma-Bologna.

Pace, A (2003) *Problematica delle libertà costituzionali*. Parte generale. Cedam, Padova.

Panella, L (2012) Il diritto dell'individuo ad una cittadinanza. *Democrazia e sicurezza – Democracy and Security Review* 2.

Panizza, S (1998) *L'introduzione dell'opinione dissenziente nel sistema di giustizia costituzionale*. Giappichelli, Torino.

Papisca, A (2013) Diritti umani: plenitudo iuris, plenitudo civitas. Ridefinire la cittadinanza alla luce del diritto della dignità umana. *La cittadinanza europea* 1.

Pegoraro, L (1987) *La Corte e il parlamento. Sentenze-indirizzo e attività legislativa*. Cedam, Padova.

Penasa, S (2009) La "ragionevolezza scientifica" delle leggi nella giurisprudenza costituzionale. *Quaderni costituzionali* 4: 817 and following.

Perassi, T (1950) *Lezioni di diritto internazionale*. Cedam, Padova.

Pérez Sola, N (2015) La incidencia de la crisis económica en las políticas de integración de la inmigración. In Gambino, S (ed) *Diritti sociali e crisi economica. Problemi e prospettive*. Giappichelli, Torino.

Pernice, I (1999) Multilevel constitutionalism and the treaty of Amsterdam: European constitution-making revisited? *Common Market Law Review* 3: 703 and following.

Polany, K (1983) *La sussistenza dell'uomo*. Einaudi, Torino.

Portinaro, P.P (1997) Dal custode della costituzione alla costituzione dei custody. In: Gozzi G (ed) *Democrazia, diritti, costituzione. I fondamenti costituzionali delle democrazie contemporanee*. Il Mulino, Bologna, p. 434 and following.

Prisco, S (1991) *Riunione (libertà di)*. Enciclopedia giuridica Treccani, vol 27, Treccani, Roma.

Prisco, S (2009) *Laicità. Un percorso di riflessione*. Giappichelli, Torino.

Quirk, W, Bridwell, R.R (1993) *Judicial Dictatorship*. Transaction Publisher, New Brunswick, London.

Rawls, J (1982) *Una teoria della giustizia*. Feltrinelli, Milano.

Ricca, M (2008) *Dike meticcia. Rotte di diritto interculturale*. Rubbettino, Catanzaro.

Ridola, P (2006) *Diritti fondamentali. Un'introduzione*. Giappichelli, Torino.

Ruggeri, A (1988) *Le attività "conseguenziali" nei rapporti fra la Corte costituzionale ed il legislatore*. Giuffrè, Milano.

Ruggeri, A (2014) Lo Stato costituzionale e le sue mutazioni genetiche. *Quaderni costituzionali* 4: 837 and following.

Ruiz-Rico Ruiz, G. (2015) El valor de los derechos constitucionales en tiempos de crisis. In: Gambino, S (ed) *Diritti sociali e crisi economica. Problemi e prospettive*. Giappichelli, Torino.

Sánchez Ferriz, R, Jimena Quesada, L (1995) *La enseñanza de los derechos humanos*. Ariel, Barcelona.

Savater, F (2003) *El valor de elegir*. Ariel, Barcelona.

Schmitt, C (1967) The Tyranny of Values. Italian edition: Accame, G (ed) (1987) *La tirannia dei valori*. Pellicani Editore, Roma.

Sen, A (2001) Eguaglianza, di che cosa? In: Carter, I (ed), *L'idea di eguaglianza*. Feltrinelli, Milano.

Silvestri, G (1981) *Le sentenze normative della Corte costituzionale*. Giurisprudenza costituzionale. Giuffrè, Milano.

Silvestri, G (2009) *Dal potere ai princìpi. Libertà ed eguaglianza nel costituzionalismo contemporaneo*. Laterza, Roma-Bari.

Stancati, P (2010) *Lo statuto costituzionale del non cittadino*. Jovene, Napoli.

Stone Sweet, A, Mathews, J (2008) Proportionality Balancing and Global Constitutionalism. *Columbia Journal of Transnational Law* 47.

Sudre, F (2009) *Droit européen et international des droits de l'homme*. PUF, Paris.

Tushnet, M (1999) *Taking the Constitution Away from the Courts*. Princeton University Press, Princeton.

UNAR (2014) *Dossier Statistico Immigrazione 2014*. Dalle discriminazioni ai diritti, Roma, IDOS, pp. 113–114.

Zagrebelsky, G (1992) *Il diritto mite*. Einaudi, Torino.

Part III

Fundamental rights in the field of intercultural research, from general theory to comparative legal analysis

4 Fundamental rights from cultural relativism to comparative legal analysis

4.1 Pluralist principle and cultural relativism

In responding to demands for an effective protection of fundamental rights in a contemporary multicultural society, an unbreakable link between constitutional theory and constitutionalism needs to be reinforced through intercultural research, even in the legal field.[1] Thus, legal studies can be very useful in promoting cultural contagion between different values, ideas, lifestyles of individuals, groups and minorities. Above all, legal studies can be useful[2] in promoting the evaluation and interpretative activity carried out with criteria beyond the literal meaning of the texts, on the one hand, and the practical function that law must develop, responding to emerging social demands and the recognition and protection of rights, on the other.

In a world where globalization is constantly on the increase, human rights cannot be recognized in a consensual way without first *de-ideologizing* human rights culture, removing its identification as a hegemonic and typical culture of the West, or as a culture in contrast to "Asian values" (Huntington 1996).[3] The recognition of multiple legal, philosophical and religious concepts inherent to different human rights cultures, as well as the cultural rights that, even today, are not recognized by the majority of contemporary States, is far more appropriate.[4] Since 1966,[5] international law has

---

1 For more analysis on the Italian experience, see (Mancini 2000, 71–86; Ricca 2008, 2013; Consorti 2013; Mazzarese 2013).
2 Those elaborated from a comparative law approach are also useful, but all lawyers, in one way or another, study law from a comparative perspective (Twining 2000 and 2007).
3 For criticism of this idea, see Sen (2011, 71; 2013, 77–78).
4 According to an interesting study by Ilenia Ruggiu (2012, 2015) only 50 constitutions, of the 190 currently existing in the world, have recognized cultural rights. Of these 50, some 30 more can be added – those that have introduced the multicultural principle or the principle of cultural diversity.
5 To this regard, see the two 1966 treaties: International Covenant on Economic, Social and Cultural Rights, articles 1, 3 and 15.1(a); International Covenant on Civil and Political Rights, Article 27, in particular.

considered culture as an element worthy of legal protection, and cultural rights as part of the human rights catalogue.

Contrary to the foundations of a constitutional State (Häberle 2001, 33), there is still clear hostility on the part of many contemporary States towards cultural pluralism and the appreciation of cultural diversity. Such hostility acts as a brake on the recognition of new rights, beginning with fundamental cultural rights, as well as the search for common principles and norms.

De-ideologizing human rights culture presupposes not only *tolerance* and respect for the *other* but also an *ethic of reciprocity* and a search for dialogue between different human rights cultures. This is not to suggest that dialogue and cross-cultural research will be a perfect (and exportable) institutional model, in other words, an objective, unique and absolute truth. In reality, there are no absolute and 'objective' values in an ontological sense – no isolated values, because each value can only reach its true meaning in conjunction with other values, and frankly, in conjunction with them all (Hartmann 1949, 408).

Nonetheless, absolute values often arise from serious biases towards those who hold different truths, or worse still, as a vindication of one's own culture. In contrast, favouring a *normative* context of openness towards moral codes and institutional structures that are different to one's own seems wise; this approach truly recognizes the incommensurability (the lack of standard of comparison) and pluralism of values,[6] institutional and social pluralism.

Intercultural research in the legal field is also advantageous for many other reasons. Even if an era of ethno-culturally homogenous States did exist, it was overtaken long ago (Choudhry 2008, 5). Today, all cultures demand equitable treatment, articulated in fundamental rights and a (multicultural) State organization, so as to clearly emphasize pluralism in both social groups and in the very sources of its legal order. As seen later, this trend is confirmed by some important constitutional experiences: the Canadian experience,[7] along with that of India, South Africa and some Latin American countries, such as Mexico where the Multicultural Constitutional State formula is used. For this reason, it would be wrong to consider pluralism and multiculturalism as opposing notions that refute each other

6 See Berlin (1958; 1988, 28–34; 1969) and Rawls (1971).
7 It is no coincidence that some of the most significant studies on the Cosmopolitan State have been written by a Canadian author, Glenn (2013). Some outstanding studies on the Canadian experience have been published in Italy, among which one can refer to Groppi (2011, 17).

(Sartori 2000, 9)[8] for this contrast reflects an epistemological misunderstanding (Pinelli 2013, 50; Mishra 2014, 62–66).

It is clear that dialogue between various cultural entities, intercultural law and the development of a multicultural State is enriched through multiplicity (similar, if you will, to microbial diversity). It is well known that maintaining biological diversity guarantees the conservation of species, ecosystems and genetic reserves – all of which are extremely important to safeguard essential ecological processes for the sake of future generations. Similarly, plurality and cultural rights are of particular interest both for the study of multicultural states and for the analysis of the dynamics of migration and the changes produced by intercultural encounters. As an example, the dynamics of migration impact not only migrants but also their 'host' within a particular 'territory' and its individual political, economic and social institutions. These impacts in turn affect the evolution of constitutional principles, inequalities and the notion of citizenship, too. Through intercultural research and the study of significant multicultural State experiences, such changes can be understood, helping integration and cohesion in multicultural societies.

This positive approach of openness and cultural respect is useful to understanding real issues and actors, through socio-cultural contextualization of normative data (Menski 2006).

Intercultural research in the legal field may, in fact, form the foundation on which institutional choices are based upon national legal systems, thus overcoming assimilationist models found most frequently in France and/or past multiculturalism models, such as those adopted in Great Britain.[9] It is no coincidence that these two models, which have been in 'crisis' for a long time, have been adopted in the two aforementioned States. The first model leans for the most part towards an abstract, sometimes even ideological, human rights universalism. The second model, despite allowing recognition and granting of certain liberty rights, discourages dialogue and forums between cultures, favouring its pragmatic political culture instead. In fact, though both models are different, they have a common root: 'assimilation' and 'separation' rely on the cultural preconception that one culture is superior to the others, which entirely goes against an *ethics of reciprocity* and intercultural research. This harsh prejudice finds its origins in colonialism

8 For a different approach to Sartori, see Morrone (2005, 24), Grosso (2006, 112), Ceccherini (2009), Baldini (2012, 1) and Amirante (2013, 135).
9 In fact, there are more models on the co-existence between immigrants and indigenous peoples, though the latter prefers an assimilationist model. For a more detailed analysis, see Rohe (2006, 58).

and in a mistaken idea of modernity, which, in its most ideological version, is at odds with foreign traditions and defends identity, with new forms of nationalism, populism and xenophobia. In order to promote dialogue, different cultures should not be judged, but interpreted and observed by those who belong to them. There can be no separation between the observer and the observed – intercultural dialogue needs an emotional involvement in order to understand and adopt the meanings of words, concepts, behaviours, norms and institutions linked to cultures. For this reason, a review of anthropology, from a pragmatic point of view, is deemed useful. According to Kant, (logical, aesthetic and moral) egoism can only be "contrasted with pluralism, which is a frame of mind in which the self, instead of being enwrapped in itself as if it were the whole world, understand and behaves itself as a mere citizen of the world" (Kant 1772). It is thanks to this way of thinking that it is possible to recognize human dignity as such. The person, as an end in him- or herself, and never understood as a means to an end, is the Kantian imperative set forth in the *Groundwork of the Metaphysic of Morals*, which was published in 1785, a few years before the French Declaration of the Rights of Man and of the Citizen (1789) and reaffirmed in the *Metaphysics of Morals*, which was published in two main parts in 1797.

Without losing its universal ethical value, dignity is relativized by enshrining it in a legal sphere. The importance of the Kantian category of dignity comes not only from its ethical but its also legal meaning – establishing, for the first time, a relation between the term 'dignity' (*Würde*) and citizen *status*. In the Kantian State theory, no person can be deprived of his or her dignity. The link between dignity and citizenship reveals the connection between dignity and rights, and it is abundantly clear how positive the introduction of human dignity in the legal world has been: it is the foundation of State community and the European constitutional realm.[10]

To avoid solipsism, and every old and new form of ethnocentrism,[11] the correct approach to interpret social phenomena, in its historical dimension, is that which derives from the combination of *cultural relativism* and *pluralist principle*. Both are acts, ways, or effects of knowledge, useful to better understand actors, processes, rules and laws/rights, according to a predominantly procedural interpretation/concept of culture (non-essentialist, not even a mere evolutionary anthropological concept, at that). Such an

10 See Häberle (1980), Ridola (2010) and Ponthoreau (2010).
11 For more on cultural relativism as corrective of ethnocentrism, see the anthropologist Boas (1911/1995). Boas highlighted the historical dimension of cultural phenomena, refuting evolutionary generalizations (Casella 2002, 40).

approach implies questioning culture as an objective, absolute and non-negotiable value. From this perspective, cultural identity, behaviour, institutions and rights cannot be seen as either 'natural' or static. Thus, in the absence of an abstract and 'universal' 'natural right', there is then no 'closed' subjective identity in its 'particularity'. Therefore, there are no 'natural' subjective rights – simply those linked to history.

A right to cultural identity is often, and rightly, invoked as a response to human rights *neocolonialism* and to theories on the 'export' of democracy. Granted, this does not mean that different cultural identities are separate worlds: the identities of individuals, groups, communities and nations arise from a relational process. For this reason, each culture is and always has been mixed (*mestizo*). This is ever more the case in today's globalized world, where not only economy and trade, but also principles, norms and human rights regularly transcend borders and cultures. From this perspective of 'cultural contamination', and not from the crystallization of differences, one can speak of a "constitutionalism of diversity"(Ghai 2000), of an "anthropology of human rights" (Baxi 2012), or rather, as argued in the following chapter, of a 'cross-cultural constitutionalism'.[12]

So, it becomes necessary to show how pluralism, understood mostly as a way of thinking, influences the study of law and rights. Above all, it is worth remembering how much law owes to legal anthropology, for it has eliminated all distinction between the individual, society and law, professing neutrality in the name of equal dignity of all cultures. Anthropologists know "the law in all its varieties, still distant in time and in its own creation" (Sacco 2007, 26). Legal anthropology is a comparative discipline that, in a way, pays attention to non-verbalized data present in the legal system.[13]

If it is true that the tools of the legal anthropologist are necessary for the study of applicable rules in traditional societies, deprived of a centralized power structure and without written law, it is equally true that said tools are useful for studying structures with a legal foundation, based on the persistent presence of uses and customs, or for the interpretation of the relationship between legal principles and rights, or in other words, between (normative) text and (social) context. This idea is especially relevant in multicultural societies, where a judicial decision may be analyzed by an

---

12 This concept was introduced for the first time in 2013. My presentation, *Diritti fondamentali, territorio e partecipazione politica nella società in rete*, was later published in Antonelli and Rossi (2014). A more detailed study on this very concept and its functions is found in Bonfiglio (2016).

13 See (MacDonald 1986; Rouland 2002; Motta 2006).

expert anthropologist with respect to the cultural practices considered 'foreign' to the local community.

This approach to legal studies is also insightful in the integration of the legal-formalistic notion of rights, according to which rights exist only if written law establishes them. In fact, it is enough to change the context and perspective[14] – different from continental European legal systems – to verify that the social function of 'validating'[15] rights is not entrusted to the law, but to the judge. Such a change would recognize and protect dormant rights: pre-existing rights in the community, though not officially recognized, would still be acknowledged, irrespective of any legislative *policy*. Dworkin qualifies these as "basic and natural rights" (Dworkin 1978).[16]

From a dynamic perspective of fundamental rights, a legal-formalistic notion makes little sense. It would be more fitting to press for a consensus on rights and their effective protection (Bobbio 1990), which would require a competent authority and procedures especially established for that purpose.

However, even for the modern natural law theory, starting with Locke, subjective (natural) rights tend to be transformed into positive rights through a social contract, instituted by consensus among all (or nearly all). Grozio[17] has already identified sources of rights in the social contract and laid down the obligation of all members to respect it through a *pars maior* consensus.

Beginning with a dynamic cultural notion and an idea of *law as a relationship* (a complex social practice), it is equally important to recognize the *diverse human rights cultures*. Nevertheless, a gradual – and sometimes very slow – convergence on common principles and a human rights core is being recognized at State, regional[18] and international levels.

---

14 In the English historical conception of rights, what makes a right effective is the possibility of seeking its protection before a court of law.
15 English catalogues of rights always invoke *former rights and freedoms of the English*.
16 In Italy, Dworkin's ideas have been widely collected, especially by Zagrebelsky and Modugno (1970, 11).
17 In 1625 Ugo Grozio wrote *De iure belli ac pacis*, in which he indicated the fundamental *praecepta* that regulated relations between individuals (see the prologue), from which the system of rights derives. The *praecepta* are understood as the fundamental principles or duties of the individual *inter homines*, which the corresponding rights are deduced from. From the *praecetum of alieni abstinentia*, that is to say, the duty not to subtract others from self-interest derives, for example, from the right of self-defense and, more generally, the recognition of a sphere of autonomy reserved equally to every person and that public authority should not interfere with.
18 See the European Convention on Human Rights (ECHR) of 1950 or the Inter-American Convention (San José de Costa Rica Convenant of 1969).

Solely on these bases, *cultural relativism* (which entails the recognition of the same dignity of cultures) and *human rights universalism* cease to be opposing ideas and instead converge on common principles, rights and duties in a field that transcends the State borders themselves. Through this convergence, *deideologization* of an abstract human rights universalism can be carried out. Both cross-breeding of cultural processes and consensual recognition of rights help build effective protection in diverse territorial areas, inasmuch as, in any case, principles capable of limiting powers and guaranteeing fundamental rights exist.

4.2 Looking East

Human rights recognition based on consensus at the international level is helpful in the prevention of any form of *human rights neo-colonialism*, which disregards the respect of any community for its own culture.[19] But this idea is also appropriate with regards to countering *human rights rhetoric*, often used by dictatorial regimes, which defines and stigmatizes underlying principles and values such as dignity, tolerance and pluralism as 'typically Western' human rights.

Amartya Sen's works often reminds us that there are historical cases in India and Turkey, as well as in Cairo and Baghdad, which "provide good examples of both the theory and practice of political and religious tolerance" (Sen 2013, 76).[20] In contrast, while in India, the sovereign Akbar, like other Mongol rulers, except Aurangzeb, spoke and practiced tolerance; in Rome, Giordano Bruno was burnt at the stake for heresy in the Field of Flowers (*Campo Dei Fiori*).

Some religions, such as Shintoism or Buddhism, are characterized by their great flexibility, going beyond the principle of tolerance. In Japan (Goodman and Refsing 1992), for example, it is perfectly normal to be both Shinto and Buddhist at the same time (Ricca 2008, 137).

In all actuality, much like the principle of tolerance, the *ethics of reciprocity*, which favours interpersonal relationships, is also present in ancient

19 Take the Universal Declaration of Human Rights of 4 July 1976, for example; see cultural rights (Articles 13, 14 and 15).
20 The problem with protection of religious minorities has been debated at length in India: there their protection is contemplated in the Right to Freedom of Religion comprised of Articles 25–28 of the Indian Constitution. Article 25 of the Constitution recognizes freedom of thought and religion, with certain limitations when certain practices and religious beliefs contradict the principle of equality which, according to the provisions of Articles 15 and 16, entails the removal of any type of discrimination based on religion, ethnicity, sex, caste, place of birth or offspring (Mahmood 1999, 93; Amirante et al. 2013).

civilizations, such as China. Confucian ethics in social relations are based on ritual norms (*li*) that require reciprocity. One example is the gift ritual, in which it is not enough, as in Western cultures, to respond with a simple 'thanks' for something that is received. Instead, it is necessary to respond by offering a gift in return. The exchange of gifts in Confucian ethics serves to maintain good relations with the *other*, to strengthen bonds between people and to preserve social order and the harmony. Harmony, of course, is understood as an ideal of justice in accordance with relationship norms, roles and socio-familial ranks (Moccia 2015, 9).

Within this system, it is incorrect to interpret submission to order and duties at the expense of freedom. For example, Confucius himself never recommended blind obedience to political authority: the truth must be spoken, even when it may offend the prince. In addition, the ability "to advise against a perverse government (when necessary and always tactfully)" (Sen 2013, 74) must never be compromised. Confucius proposed a government based on human virtues, in tune with rites and traditions linked to ancient wisdom traditions of the Xia dynasty.

There is little opportunity in Chinese culture, even today, to innovate or to break with tradition. For this reason, it is important that in China a greater focus is gradually emerging on liberty rights and the introduction of the rule of law (Buyun 1980; Lie and Xiaoqing 2006). This has been clear since the 1982 constitution, which has been amended on numerous occasions, notably that of 2004, which in Article 33 provides human rights protection and in Article 13, the protection of private property. While it is true that this constitution is still emerging, a debate began in 2008[21] in China concerning the urgency of amending constitutional provisions, setting up a true system of constitutional review (Hui 2015, 39) and applying the constitution, through "constitutional judicialization" (Lie 2006, 240–245; Hui 2015, 47).

Despite these interesting and recent developments, a number of unresolved issues remain in China, among them, the Tibetan issue. Over time, this issue has not only highlighted a problem of independence, but also a lack of respect for human rights.

Asia's other giant, India, shows very different features – either because of its particular legal tradition (Lingat 2003; Sharma 2015)[22] or because today it constitutes a "model" (Mahajan 2005), or rather a 'prototype' of

---

21 In this context, the Chinese Political Constitutionalist School (PCS) seems relevant (Quanxi 2015, 17).

22 Singh (1985) is relevant. Here, the author raises a Kantian notion of law as *dharma* which is of great interest: the notion of the German philosophy, 'regulative idea', is found in the Indian philosophy's concept of *dharma*. For more on Singh's work, see Baxi (2014, 5–24). For a synthetic introduction to India's legal system, see Acquarone (2015).

a true multicultural State,[23] wherein six great religions (Hinduism, Buddhism, Jainism, Islam, Christianity and Sikhism)[24] co-exist, and an incredible 1,576 languages or dialects (grouped into main languages, 22 of which are officially recognized) are spoken. In the Indian Federation, the constitutional principle of equality, embodied in different forms and modalities with respect to Western legal traditions (Saraswati 2002, 18), has favoured individual and lower-class political participation, contradicting India's legal tradition and its *Varna* social code (i.e. the caste system in which inequality is legitimate). For this reason, it can be said that the 'constitutional fathers' of India bravely challenged the caste system, recognizing and guaranteeing fundamental rights, through the confirmation of the principles of equality and freedom. Similarly, the Indian Constitution, drawn up in the years after World War II, was "genetically" and substantially multicultural, assessing cultural and social differences and adopting precise institutional measures with a view to recognizing the cultures of the different communities.[25] Thus, many separatist claims have been superseded by the recognition of political subjectivity of many linguistic and cultural communities (Amirante 2014, 61). This has also been a result of constitutional reforms, establishing a number of linguistic states, thus modifying the internal territorial organization of India.

In India, we find a constitutional experience that goes beyond the limits of liberal multiculturalism and reaffirms a "democratic multiculturalism" founded upon the recognition of cultural diversity, not only in terms of the protection of individual rights, but also through the political involvement of social groups and community as a whole (Bhargava 1999, 2012).

In both India and China, a deep-rooted tension is evident between constitutional norms and social reality, traditionally linked to rules and practices that are clearly opposed to constitutionally recognized principles and fundamental rights.[26] One striking example is the violation of women's rights, which are constitutionally recognized but often not applied. Practices such

23 On the debate surrounding multiculturalism as a legal doctrine and a specific constitutional policy, see Kimlycka (2005, 22–55), Amirante (2011, 31), Amirante (2014, 62) and Amirante (2015, 11–46).
24 For more on issues relating to religious pluralism, see Derrett (1968).
25 See Bhattacharyya (2003, 152), Chandra and Mahajan (2007), Mahajan (2013, 98) and Mishra and Bharath (2014, 62–66).
26 The 1950 Constitution of India establishes the principle of gender equality in its Preamble, in both the Fundamental Rights and Fundamental Duties Articles, and also in the Article on Guiding Principles of State Policy. In this regard, there can be no discrimination on the part of the State based on sex (Article 15.1), and nothing prevents the State from providing specific measures for women and children (Article 15.3). Similarly, in the area of Criminal and Labour Law, positive discrimination measures have been envisaged for women, and

as female infanticide or selective abortion have not yet been eliminated, and the percentage of early marriages or 'girl-wives' is still very high. Similarly, and despite being banned by law and condemned by the India's Supreme Court, crimes of honour are still widespread.

4.3 Looking to the African continent

Moving from the Asian to the African continent, various interesting examples show evidence of African originality, even in the field of human rights. Here, reflections on decentralized, stateless societies (though not necessarily without law), on the founding principles of traditional law, and on the very different way of conceiving relations between the individual member and his or her group (Sacco 2009, 96), contribute to the construction of an African theory of law (Mougnonzo 2007). This legal construction is by no means abstract, and its origins lie in the study of specific cases and in the recognition of the indissoluble nature of civil, political, economic, social and cultural rights, as derived from the African Charter on Human and People's Rights.[27]

While both political changes stemming from the "Arab Spring" (El Houssi 2013, 61–92) and the adoption of the 2014 constitution in Tunisia are important, in terms of constitutional processes,[28] the most consolidated constitutional experience in the African continent, from the point of view of fundamental rights recognition and, in particular, of cultural rights recognition, can be found in South Africa (Hughes 2014, 115–301).[29]

Unlike other African States which forced the modernization of their formal legal and institutional systems, South Africa, following its independence,

---

these have been confirmed by the courts, in compliance with the aforementioned constitutional mandate.

27 The Charter, adopted at the 1981 Conference of Heads of State and Government of the United States, came into force in 1986, having met the required number of ratifications. Human rights recognized by the African Charter are civil and political, as well as economic and social. It is the first international human rights convention that recognizes the rights of peoples (i.e. the right to equality of all peoples, the right to self-determination, the right to own natural resources, the right to development and the right to a healthy environment). It is also the first legally binding instrument of international law expressly relating to rights and duties. The African Charter provides *inter alia* for the individual's duty to family, society and the international community, as well as the duty not to discriminate, the duty to maintain parents in cases of need, the duty to work to the fullest of their abilities, and the duty to preserve and strengthen positive African cultural values.

28 There has even been talk of a model of "participatory constitutionalism". On this subject, see Khatib (2013, 315–340).

29 Among Italian studies, the following are also relevant: Dau (2011), Dau (2012), Federico (2009), Orrù (1998), Scaffardi (1996) and Pegoraro and Rinella (1997).

moved towards its indigenous legal system in assessing institutional plurality and especially linguistic pluralism.

Recognition and respect for linguistic pluralism[30] is set out in the 1996 Constitution (Articles 6, 9.3, 30 and 31). Apart from recognizing the historically reduced use and status of indigenous languages, the State undertakes to raise their *status* and promote their use (Article 6.2). To this end, the constitution provides for the creation, through a national act, of a Pan South African Language Board whose functions are "(a) promote, and create conditions for, the development and use of all official languages, the Khoi, Nama and San languages, and sign languages; (b) promote and ensure respect for all languages commonly used by communities in South Africa, including German, Greek, Gujarati, Hindi, Portuguese, Tamil, Telegu and Urdu, and Arabic, Hebrew, Sanskrit and other languages used for religious purposes in South Africa" (Article 6.5).

The right to use one's own language, and to participate in the cultural life that one chooses, is recognized as an individual right (Article 30) and also as a right of cultural, religious and linguistic communities (Article 31).[31] Also, the exercise of these (individual and collective) rights cannot violate any provision of the Bill of Rights (Article 31, 2), in accordance with the democratic values of human dignity, equality and freedom. Ultimately, despite recognizing cultural rights, there is as such a preference for the protection of individuals versus groups. Article 39, which provides for the interpretation of the Bill of Rights, confirms this: "A court, tribunal or forum must promote the values that underlie an open and democratic society based on human dignity, equality and freedom, must consider international law; and may consider foreign law". Similarly, in interpreting each law and in developing *common law* and traditional law rules, courts and forums must promote the spirit, meaning and purpose of the Bill of Rights. The Bill of Rights does not prevent the existence of other rights or freedoms recognized by *common law* rules, traditional laws or by an act, as long as they conform to the bill itself.

Therefore, Article 39, which regulates the interpretation of the Bill of Rights, should be taken into account when analysing Title XII of the South African constitution, which, in turn, recognizes both traditional law and

---

30 According to Article 6.1, there are 11 official languages: Sepedi, Sesotho, Setswana, siSwati, Tshivenda, Xitsonga, Afrikáans, English, isiNdebele, isiXhosa and isiZulu.

31 Article 31 states: "(1) Persons belonging to a cultural, religious or linguistic community may not be denied the right, with other members of that community – (a). to enjoy their culture, practise their religion and use their language; and – (b). to form, join and maintain cultural, religious and linguistic associations and other organs of civil society. (2) The rights in subArticle (1) may not be exercised in a manner inconsistent with any provision of the Bill of Rights".

traditional rights, and whose limit is in the fundamental rights catalogue provided for in the Bill of Rights itself. This catalogue is to be understood as open-ended, given that, as aforementioned, it *must* respect public international law rules and *may* even take into account foreign law. In short, traditional communities have a right to 'self-legitimation', though their uses and customs must confirm to the principles contained in the Bill of Rights.

Hence various, diverse traditional legal systems become part of a cultural and institutional mosaic, which within a framework of respect for the fundamental principles and rights enshrined in the 1996 Constitution and the 2003 *Traditional Leadership and Governance Framework Bill*, finds itself reconstituted and part of a united order, sustained by a spirit of inclusion and reciprocal hybridization.

4.4 Looking to Latin American countries

Within the framework of Latin American countries, mixed (*mestizo*) populations (that is, with European and indigenous genetic heritages) are in many instances, the majority (constituting more than 50% of the total population).[32] For this reason, the 2008 Ecuadorian Constitution and the 2009 Bolivian Constitution deserve special attention. Under these constitutional systems, institutional State organization based on a solidarity and sustainable development model prevails. This model is characterized by three elements: *Good Living*, legal recognition of rights of nature and plurinationality.

The first two elements go beyond Western anthropocentric ideals and take a subjective view of nature with respect to human beings, according to Andean cosmology. This world view respects Andean indigenous tradition, with common resources and the rights of future generations (Article 33, Bolivian Constitution). The legal recognition of the rights of nature means that, in both legal systems, nature goes from being an 'object' to a 'subject', a holder of legal interests. A peculiar difference can be found in Ecuador, where nature's subjective sphere is constitutional, while in Bolivia this recognition is provided by ordinary legislation.

The third element – plurinationality – is explicitly mentioned in Article 1 of the Bolivian Constitution, which also characterizes the State in a social, democratic and intercultural sense. Bolivia is founded on plurality and political, economic, juridical, cultural and linguistic[33] pluralism in order to favour the country's integration process.

---

32 Notably, Mexico, Panama, Colombia, Honduras, Venezuela and Paraguay.
33 Article 5.1 recognizes the State's official languages: Spanish and all the languages spoken by indigenous peoples and nations (Aymara, Araona, Baure, Bésiro, Canichana, Cavineño, Cayubaba, Chácobo, Chimán, Ese Ejja, Guaraní, Guarasu'we, Guarayu, Itonama,

Among the emerging countries of Latin America, Brazil, Chile[34] and Mexico are worth special mention, given that according to the *Global Competitiveness Report*, they have the most competitive economies. However, serious social inequalities existing in these countries, representing a major obstacle to the development and rational use of the human and natural resources at their disposal.[35]

Out of the three States, Mexico is the only one that can be considered a pluricultural State governed by the rule of law (Gonzáles 1997, 169–190).[36] The first constitutional review procedure that led to the amendment of Article 4 was carried out in 1992, establishing the pluricultural nature of the Mexican nation.[37] However, it was not until the 2001 amendment that the rights of indigenous peoples were more specifically recognized in the newly drafted Article 2, together with the limits they are subject to: general principles enshrined in the constitution, the respect for individual guarantees, human rights and, especially, the dignity and integrity of women.

Article 2 of the Mexican Constitution recognizes internal normative systems of indigenous peoples as sources of law, and indigenous courts as part of the judiciary.[38] This evolution of the Mexican State has led to the abandonment of paternalistic legal protectionism and a transformation of the political organization: it has become a multicultural State. This has led, for example, to the recognition of permanent seats for indigenous peoples in legislative bodies at federal, local and municipal levels (Rea 2015, 1083–1117).

Leco, Machajuyai-Kallawaya, Machineri, Maropa, Mojeño-Trinitario, Mojeño-Ignaciano, Moré, Mosetén, Movima, Pacawara, Puquina, Quechua, Sirionó, Tacana, Tapiete, Toromona, Uru-Chipaya, Weenhayek, Yaminawa, Yuki, Yuracaré and Zamuco).

34 See www.leychile.cl/Navegar?idNorma=242302.

35 The irrational use of natural resources does not respect the 1988 Brazilian Constitution, which recognizes, in Article 225, the right of everyone to an ecologically balanced environment, which is a public good for the people's use and essential for a healthy life. The government and the community have a duty to defend and to preserve the environment for present and future generations. In the Brazilian Constitution, lands traditionally occupied by the Indians are considered as common property, owned collectively and protected by the Federal Union (Article 20). Also, according to Article 231, Indians' social organization, customs, languages, creeds and traditions, as well as their original rights to the lands they traditionally occupy, are recognized. Additionally, there is a constitutional duty of the State to delineate these lands and protect and ensure respect for their property.

36 On Mexico as a cross-cultural (*mestisation*) laboratory, see what is now considered a classical inter-American study: Gruzinski (1988).

37 See Carducci and Estrada (1998) and Olivetti (2013, 177).

38 See Article 2(A) of the Mexican Constitution.

4.5 The dual nature of the dignity–rights relationship: some examples

As is clear from the evidence presented earlier, respect for the *other*, for an ethics of reciprocity, tolerance, solidarity, freedom, equality, political and cultural pluralism, as well as individual rights and collective rights, all represent the common denominator for different human rights cultures. This common ground is the starting point to cultivate, through intercultural dialogue, the value of human dignity (both in its social and economic dimension), whose ethical and legal content is ever-changing in space and time.

If 'natural' rights are endowed with empirical content, yet camouflaged as universal, then a human rights culture that is unable to *de-ideologize* falsely 'natural' content seems important. In this way, by placing the individual in his or her 'effective' reality, the historical and cultural recognition of rights is carried out through a legal confirmation of the rights themselves, in order to favour their effective protection.

As previously mentioned, it is a question of the shared transformation of 'natural rights' into fundamental rights, adopted and set down by positive legal systems. In fact, this transformation is not natural at all, but rather is of a cultural and historical nature. Therefore, this transformation gradually takes place everywhere. It is worth noting, for instance, the contradiction between the right to life and the death penalty, still present today – even in liberal-democratic legal frameworks.

If a social contract, or a constitutional pact, must guarantee at least one natural right (Hobbes) – i.e. the right to individual life – how can the legislative rationale prevail over this fundamental right? The death penalty cannot be justified in the name of the State, its sovereignty or its legislative rationale, by considering (Rea 2015, 1083–1117) some crimes[39] "worthy of death", as Kant pointed out. The ethical and legal value of human dignity is in no way compatible with the death penalty, despite the fact that today, some States still consider some crimes 'punishable by death'.

Without resorting to the right-to-life rhetoric, Cesare Beccaria asks himself in his *Essay on Crimes and Punishments* (1764),[40] "what right, I ask, have men to cut the throats of their fellow-creatures?", and specifies that it is certainly

---

39 Kant, in *The Metaphysics of Morals*, passionately defends the death penalty, and disagrees with Beccaria, who considers it illegal in his famous treatise *On Crimes and Punishments*.

40 The quotes are taken from the fifteenth edition of the "Universale Economica" – I Classici della Feltrinelli, Milano, 2009.

not that on which the sovereignty and laws are founded. The laws, as I have said before, are only the sum of the smallest portions of the private liberty of each individual, and represent the general will, which is the aggregate of that of each individual.

In his essay, Beccaria affirms – within a reformist approach of Legal Enlightenment – that the death penalty is most certainly not a *right*. He adds that "in a reign of [legal] tranquillity" it is neither useful nor necessary – because death as a spectacle or an object of compassion mixed with displeasure does not put a curb on crimes. On the contrary, as he highlights, "death is a terrible but momentary spectacle, and therefore, a less efficacious method of deterring others, than the continued example of a man deprived of his liberty". Indeed, the deprivation of liberty constitutes a "powerful preventive" (the strongest deterrent to commit crimes). Undoubtedly, Beccaria's Legal Enlightenment is influenced by Helvétius's French utilitarianism, fighting against legislative ignorance by considering individual interests contrary to the general interest. His was an empirical approach to foster an extension of rights. Bentham also learned this utilitarianism from Helvetius, which he later proposed in England via radical reform, opposing utility and natural rights.

Beccaria's message was well received in Italy and in the European public sphere. It was accepted despite the fact that Beccaria did not exclude the application of the death penalty in two specific cases,[41] even though the right to life implies no exceptions to the absolute ban on the death penalty. This ban is not recognized by any American legal framework, although it is worth noting that, little by little, the US Supreme Court influence regarding the interpretation of Amendment VIII ("Nor cruel and unusual punishment [shall] be inflicted") is in line with the exclusion of the death penalty (Strauss 2009, 859). It has also emphasized that "thirty states rejected the juvenile death penalty, including eighteen that allowed the death penalty in other circumstances".[42]

In Italian Constitutional Act 1/2007, the prohibition of the death penalty must be understood in an absolute manner and without exception. Before the amendment, paragraph 4 of Article 27 Italian Constitution stated that the

41 "The death of a citizen cannot be necessary except in one case. When, even though he is deprived of his liberty, he has such power and connections as may endanger the security of the nation; when his existence may produce a dangerous revolution in the established form of government. But even in this case, it can only be necessary when a nation is on the verge of recovering or losing its liberty; or in times of absolute anarchy, when the disorders themselves hold the place of laws" (Beccaria 1764, 80).
42 See, for example, *Roper v Simmons*, 543 US Supreme Court (2005, 559–560).

death penalty was not allowed "except in cases provided for by military laws in times of war". In the case of domestic law, an absolute prohibition does not pose problems, but rather reinforces what is established by Article 1 of Act 589/1994 for offences stated in the Military Criminal Code of War and military war legislation, which sets out the abolition of the death penalty and its replacement by the maximum penalty provided for in the Criminal Code.

Similarly, in the European arena, this trend is confirmed, not only after the entry into force on 1 July 2003 of Protocol 13 of the European Convention on Human Rights (ECHR) – which expressly abolished the death penalty in all circumstances, even in times of war or imminent threat of war – but also through Article 2.2 of the Charter of Fundamental Rights of the European Union: "No one shall be condemned to the death penalty, or executed".

However, outside the European constitutional field, a ban on the death penalty poses some sobering issues in relation to States requesting extradition for a crime punishable by death. Undoubtedly, extradition to such States must be considered contrary to the Italian Constitution and the principles and values it represents, the main of which would be life as the most essential legal interest.[43] Italy may stipulate extradition agreements or treaties only in cases in which the foreign law provides for an automatic substitution of the death penalty.

Similarly, and as ratified by the Strasbourg Court on numerous occasions, Article 2 of the ECHR states that States have a negative obligation not to deprive their citizens of the right to life, and also to take appropriate and positive measures to protect the life of those under their jurisdiction.[44] Taking this into account, it is clear that there is a violation of Article 2 of the ECHR not only by directly depriving people of their lives, but also when the State fails to take measures to avoid specific risks to people's lives, in particular when they are easily preventable.

43 The Strasbourg Court has declared Article 698, paragraph 2 of the Criminal Procedure Code and Act 225/1984 unconstitutional, given that it complies with the 1984 Treaty signed with the United States, in which the prohibition of capital punishment set out in Article 27, paragraph 4 of the Italian Constitution imposes an absolute guarantee and is not subject to "sufficient guarantees" of the requesting order.
44 See the controversial case *Giuliani v Italy*, in which the Court concluded that Article 2.1 "enjoins the State not only to refrain from the intentional and unlawful taking of life, but also to take appropriate steps to safeguard the lives of those within its jurisdiction". See European Court of Human Rights, *Giuliani and Gaggio v Italy*, 24 March 2011, case 23458/02, paragraph 208. Also see *L.C.B. v the United Kingdom*, 9 June 1998, case 14/1997/798/1001, paragraph 36; *Osman v the United Kingdom*, 28 October 1998, case 87/1997/871/1083, parararagraph 115; *Makaratzis v Greece*, 20 December 2004, case 50385/99, paragraph 57–59; *Nachova and others v Bulgaria*, 6 July 2005, cases 43577/98 and 43579/98, paragraph 96.

From this first example, one can infer that the extension and effective protection of fundamental rights are changing parameters in time and space. These changes depend on the direct relationship between the notions of dignity and rights themselves, in which the very content of rights, their evolution and their extension to individuals, collectives and different communities is transformed.

If human dignity, as a supreme value, constitutes the basic foundation of the principles of liberty and equality, as well as civil, political and social rights, then not all fundamental rights stem from the individual personal ethics to which we reasonably attach great weight in the frame of traditional Western thought. Instead, some rights originate from the recognition of collective rights – the right to the environment, the right to development and cultural rights (Vasak 1982), for example – that are all considered as fundamental rights. However, from a historical and legal standpoint, one can understand why the legal recognition of first- and second-generation fundamental rights has been a somewhat gradual process.

For example, in a constitutional (liberal) State, legal subjectivity is recognized but also regulated by distinguishing between *legal personality* and *legal capacity* (ability to act). This, in turn, might explain the exclusion of women, and of many other human beings, given their supposedly reduced capacity to act, much like 'minors' and, therefore, why such groups are deprived of essential political, civil and social rights.

As a matter of fact, the direct relationship between dignity and rights is of particular interest if analyzed from the perspective of a gradual affirmation of the gender equality principle. For example, the human rights catalogues of the late eighteenth century, before the American and subsequent to the French Bill of Rights, do not mention women as potential rights holders – granting rights only to their male counterparts. Constitutionalists at that time believed that women, given their "natural" (or biological) difference, should be limited to the private sphere, whereas men by their 'natural' rational – rather than emotional – "nature" were destined to act in the public sphere.

For a substantial part of the nineteenth and the early part of the twentieth centuries, women did not have the right to vote. Britain was the first country to grant women the right to vote in administrative elections in the second half of the nineteenth century and for specific policies in 1918. In Italy, the 1861 Electoral Act excluded the rights to vote and to stand for election on the basis of illiteracy, sex (women), disability and criminal conviction (detainees). It was not until 1946 that women acquired the right to vote in Italy. Incidentally, the last European country to recognize women's right to vote was Switzerland, in 1971.

Compared to eighteenth-century bills of rights, the Universal Declaration of Human Rights of 1948 and the democratic constitutions of the post–World

War II period prohibit any discrimination based on sex and establish equal rights for men and women. However, discrimination and violence against women remain common. This is why the 1979 Convention on the Elimination of All Forms of Discrimination against Women (CEDAW) establishes that, despite the recognition of the gender equality principle, the realization of women's rights requires States to adopt appropriate measures, beginning with the elimination of rules that are manifestly contrary to the principle of equality and to the value of the human dignity.

One example of why such measures are so necessary is the fact that, until the beginning of the 1980s,[45] the Italian Criminal Code provided for a "crime of honour" and recognized the practice of "restorative marriage". This practice allowed the possibility of suppressing a crime of sexual violence, including injuries to minors, if such conduct was followed by a so-called restorative marriage between the accused and the victim, thus saving the accused's honour and that of the family. Similarly, rape was considered a crime "against morality" and not "against the individual".[46]

It is useful to highlight that practices, norms and real crimes that were previously relegated to the shelves of social and legal archaeology are now somehow resurfacing, albeit related to different cultural models. This phenomenon should not be downplayed and, even in multicultural societies, can be channelled, especially from a prevention, integration and social cohesion standpoint. On a repressive level, there is a possibility that domestic abuse can be justified by the abuser invoking, as a defensive strategy, the diversity of their cultural model. Even in a multicultural society, the answer to this question must be that, where the level of violence breaches fundamental rights, such as life and physical integrity, cultural diversity that prompts the commission of a particular offence cannot exonerate or mitigate liability.

There are practices, such as female genital mutilation, which have captured the attention of Western countries, especially with contemporary migratory flows. In many African communities, mutilation represents an element of social integration, rather than isolation or discrimination. However, for African women and girls living in European societies, genital mutilation is a stigma and a major obstacle to social integration. This practice also limits their individual autonomy. Although this is not penalized in African countries, it is prohibited in countries where it constitutes not only an obstacle to integration and social cohesion, but above all, a violation

---

45 The aforementioned acts were repealed by Act 442 of 1981. Also, until Constitutional Court Judgement 126/1968, the Criminal Code provided for the punishment of adultery carried out by women, but not that of the husband or of his concubine.

46 Up until Act 66/1996 of 15 February, Sexual Offences Act. Translator's note: law against sexual violence.

of fundamental rights. Some States, such as Italy, choose to develop *ad hoc* regulations, particularly in the area of prevention through information campaigns, and targeting immigrants from countries where such practices are carried out, effectively bringing such issues to the core of political debate. This is beneficial because it publicly values its cultural significance, enabling the participation of a plurality of subjects (volunteer organizations, non-profits, health structures, schools, etc.) in potential prevention programs.[47]

Therefore, socio-cultural contextualization of such norms and practices is important to understand the complex relationship between dignity and rights. The value of human dignity, in the context of its evolution from an ethical to a legal category, changes its meaning depending on the 'constitutional order'.[48]

The value of human dignity is also linked to the concept of citizenship and, above all, the recognition and guarantee of fundamental rights. Such changes occurred in people's consciousness even before countless written constitutions were drafted. The *positive* (legal) content of a historically determined dignity – or in other words, the meaning that dignity assumes with implementation of fundamental and institutional principles – depends on a variety of factors: historical dynamics, the balance between opposing interests, changes in customs, cultural mediation, conflict and social policies. For instance, if welfare benefits are insufficient, to the point where the European Union could break down in the absence of a *European welfare*, it is unlikely that all citizens (Germans and Greeks alike) will have the same social dignity. Furthermore, if the level of jurisdictional protection of social rights is far less than that enjoyed by civil rights guarantees, because of its supposed budgetary link, this will impede full human development. Development itself depends on individual capacities that reflect a freedom of choice between different alternatives within an ideal *welfare* system that promotes equal capacities: i.e. the right to education.

The direct relationship between dignity and rights means that both possess a precise *legal content*. Fundamental rights, above all, can change depending on the location and time setting. For example, in a given context, private property (the right of exclusive property) may be "a terrible, and

---

47 As a matter of fact, with Act 7/2006, the Italian legislature not only prohibited such practices but also introduced a measure to prevent female genital mutilation (clitoridectomy, infibulation and any other practices which had the same effects).

48 According to Barbera (2015, 267) "the political and social as well as the political and cultural contexts, whereby recognition of fundamental constitutional principles takes place is precisely where different norms are needed. Social order modelled with the aims and values of the political, social and cultural forces that are recognised in these texts".

perhaps unnecessary right" when it has left nothing "but a bare existence" (Beccaria 1764, 71). Likewise, in the transition from nineteenth-century liberal constitutions to those promulgated after World War II, the same private property considered as an inviolable right – such as was the case of the Albertine Statute – became officially recognized by the Italian Constitution and guaranteed by law, so as to "ensure its social function and make it accessible to all". In this regard, it could be expropriated for reasons of general interest only in cases agreed by the law and with provisions for compensation (Article 42, Italian Constitution).

Fundamental rights may even change because of the influence of scientific and technological research within social dynamics. The evolution of the right to privacy provides us with a good example of this. At the end of the nineteenth century, the *right of privacy*, according to the theory set out by Warren and Brandeis's remarkable article (Warren and Brandeis 1890, 193), was understood as the *right to be alone*. Its origin lies in industrial society and arises from the desire of the people and, above all, the bourgeoisie, to defend their privacy and family life against press interference. The right to privacy was, at that time, defined as a negative right, a claim to preserve the privacy of the family environment against external interferences. With the advent of post–World War II social and democratic States, this individualistic approach of the right to privacy evolved. It no longer represented a mere *negative freedom*, by which the State refrained from acts that could deny or restrict individual freedom, but was constituted also as a functional right, relating to the free development of the person. In this regard, we have moved from an individualistic conception of the right to privacy to a social one, which underlies the need for a legal framework that binds the State to promote participation and control of the interested parties. Subsequently, *digital society* has created a right to privacy[49] with an entirely different meaning: it has taken on a greater dimension, not only beyond the home,[50] but also beyond a territorial scope. Nowadays, 'network society' presents itself as a great opportunity for the exercise of fundamental

---

49 The debate concerning its legal nature, from the point of view of the general theory of subjective rights, has been very fruitful in the past. Consider the discussion of 'rights of personality', between monistic and pluralistic theories. Another approach on privacy points to the possibility that these rights are used economically by their owners, given the widespread practice of commodifying the features of personality (Resta 2000, 299). Other considerations on the legal nature of privacy are expressed in the framework of 'obscuring' subjective law theory. This legal fog approach can be seen, for example, in Perlingieri, who has stated that human beings should be understood in a unitary way, not as rights but as a values. (Perlingieri 1972, 186). For a deeper analysis on privacy issues, see Ubertazzi (2004).

50 See Rallo and García (2015) and Resta and Zeno-Zencovich (2015).

rights that transform individuals into citizens (Rousseau 2015): freedom of thought and expression and attempts to block the media, for example. Network society can also contribute in promoting citizen participation through public consultations, assessing institutions of direct democracy, including at European level,[51] allowing for a greater transparency in decision-making processes, in supervising public authorities and in improving accountability procedures (Gutwirth and De Hert 2010, 271). However, the free network faces opposition from those States with authoritarian legal orders that qualify allegations of human rights violations, as well as confrontation between cultures based on different values, as dangerous. Beyond State territorial limits, 'citizenship' in the online world offers many opportunities for liberty rights and freedom in general, though it may create new forms of inequality if a 'right to technology' is not guaranteed for all: it will be vital to establish universal access to the Internet as a fundamental right of the person, understood as a common legal interest.

In addition, it is worth remembering that scientific and technological innovation raises new issues that create dissent and lead to a reconsideration of legal categories,[52] since innovation itself can create new forms of inequality. Artificial fertilization techniques, or even the case of surrogate motherhood, can be used as examples. The latter is considered one of the most controversial practices in this field, as it foregoes the *mater semper certa est* principle. If the interests and rights of the persons involved in this practice are considered (parents, surrogate mother and child), it seems certain that each will experience vulnerability. Among the various issues affecting the parents are reproductive rights in relation to reproductive and sexual health, infertility treatment, and the ban on making the human body or its parts a source of financial gain.[53] As for the surrogate mother, in some socio-cultural contexts she can reinforce and cause gender inequalities.

51 Participation in the Treaty of Lisbon is specifically reflected in Article 11.4 by the citizens' initiative, through which one million citizens, belonging to a significant number of Member States, can go directly to the European Commission and present a bill that defends their interests in one of the areas of competence of the European Union. This standard – with the establishment of a one-year period for the collection of "statements of support" (i.e. a minimum number of signatures) – allows signatures to be collected not only on paper, but also electronically, through a system certified by a national authority. Also, in order to facilitate the organizational committee, the Commission has developed an open software program that can be used by promoters to solicit online statements of support.

52 For an interesting BioLaw introduction from a Comparative Law approach, see Casonato (2012).

53 The Oviedo Convention for the Protection of Human Rights and Dignity of the Human Being with regard to the Application of Biology and Medicine (Convention on Human Rights and Biomedicine) and the Charter of Fundamental Rights of the European Union

In relation to the child born through surrogacy, he or she can be pushed to a somewhat secondary position regarding the agreement between the parents/clients and the pregnant mother/provider; this situation should be especially protected by the principle of the best interests of the child. One of the most critical aspects related to this practice is the legal recognition of the relationship ('parentage') between the child born of gestational surrogacy and the parents/clients. The problem stems from the choice of applicable law controversy between the country of birth and the child's country of destination. However, in accordance with the case law of the European Court of Human Rights,[54] such a clash should not compromise the need to (always) ensure effective protection of the child, even if said practice – at least in its *profitable* version – is not recognized by international or European law.

Many other examples could be analyzed (i.e. the right to a dignified death; the right to a sex change, even without reassignment surgery; and so forth),[55] which would confirm not only the complexity and the dynamism of the relationship between dignity and rights, but also the notion of the law as a complex social practice and a historical-cultural experience.

References

Acquarone, L (2015) *Tra Dharma, Common Law e WTO*. Edizioni Unicopli, Milano.
Amirante, D (2011) The Indian Multicultural State: un Model for Asia or More? In: Amirante, D, Pepe, V (eds) *Stato democratico e società multiculturale. Dalla tutela delle minoranze al riconoscimento delle diversità culturali*. Giappichelli, Torino.
Amirante, D (2013) Origini, struttura e caratteri generali della Costituzione indiana. In: Amirante, D, Decaro, C, Pföstl, E (eds) *La Costituzione dell'Unione Indiana*. Giappichelli, Torino.
Amirante, D (2014) *Lo Stato multiculturale. Contributo alla teoria dello Stato dalla prospettiva dell'Unione Indiana*. Bononia University Press, Bologna.
Amirante, D (2015) Al di là dell'Occidente. Sfide epistemologiche e spunti euristici nella comparazione "verso Oriente". *Diritto pubblico comparato ed europeo* 1: 11–46.
Antonelli, F, Rossi, E (eds) (2014) *Homo Dignus. Cittadinanza, democrazia e diritti in un mondo in trasformazione*. Cedam, Padova.
Baldini, V (2012) Diritto, pluralismo culturale, Costituzione. La prospettiva storico-filosofica quale 'precomprensione' per l'interpretazione dei 'valori' costituzionali. In: Baldini, V (ed) *Multiculturalismo*. Cedam, Padova.

---

establish, in Articles 21 and 3, respectively, the prohibition of financial gain and disposal of any human body or part thereof.
54 ECHR *Mennesson v France, Labassee v France, CJEU D. and others v Belgium*, and *Paradiso and Campanelli v Italy*.
55 See, in addition, the Italian Supreme Court Judgement 15138/2015 on sex change without surgical intervention, whereby 'self-perception', 'social role' and the change of 'socio-cultural perspective' are highlighted.

Barghava, R (2012) *What Is Political Theory and Why We Need It*. Oxford Collected Essays, New Delhi.

Baxi, U (2012) *The Future of Human Rights*. Oxford University Press, New Delhi.

Baxi, U (2014) Chhtrapati Singh and the Idea of a Legal Theory. *Journal of the Indian Law Institute* 1: 5–24.

Beccaria, C (1764) Dei delitti e delle pene. Italian edition: (2009) *"Universale Economica" – I*. Classici della Feltrinelli, Milano.

Berlin, I (1958) Two Concepts of Liberty. Italian edition: (2000) *Due concetti di libertà*. Feltrinelli, Milano.

Berlin, I (1969) Introduction: Four Essays on Liberty. Italian edition: Hardy, H, Ricciardi, M (eds) (2010) *Introduzione in Id., Libertà*. Feltrinelli, Milano.

Berlin, I (1988) The Search for Ideal. Italian edition: *La ricerca dell'ideale*. In: Hardy, H (ed) (1994) Id., *Il legno storto dell'umanità. Capitoli di storia delle idee*. Adelphi, Milano, pp. 28–34.

Bhargava, R (1999) Introducing Multiculturalism. In: Bhargava, R, Bagchi, A.K, Sudarshan, R (eds) *Multiculturalism, Liberalism and Democracy*, Oxford University Press, Delhi.

Bhattacharyya, H (2003) Multiculturalism in contemporary India. *International Journal on Multicultural Societies (IJMS)* 2.

Boas, F (1911) The Mind of Primitive Man. Italian edition: (1995) *L'uomo primitivo*. Laterza, Roma-Bari.

Bobbio, N (1990) *L'età dei diritti*. Einaudi, Torino.

Bonfiglio, S (2016) Per una teoria interculturale dei diritti fondamentali e della Costituzione. *Diritto pubblico comparato ed europeo* 1.

Buyun, L (1980) Can Rule of Law Be Combined with Rule of Man? *CASS Journal of Law* 2.

Carducci, M, Estrada Aguilar, R (1998) *Le riforme costituzionali in Messico: 1917–1997*. Prensa Multimedia, Lecce.

Casella, A (2002) *Paltrinieri, Lineamenti essenziali di storia dell'antropologia culturale*. EDUCatt Università Cattolica, Milano.

Casonato, C (2012) *Introduzione al biodiritto*. Giappichelli, Torino.

Ceccherini, E (2009) *Voce Multiculturalismo*. Digesto, Torino.

Chandra, B, Mahajan, S (eds) (2007) *Composite Culture in a Multicultural Society*. Pearson Longman, New Delhi.

Choudhry, S (2008) Bridging Comparative Politics and Comparative Constitutional Law: Constitutional Design in Divided Societies. In: Choudhry, S (ed) *Constitutional Design for Divided Societies: Integration or Accommodation?* New York: Oxford University Press.

Consorti, P (2013) *Conflitti mediazione e diritto interculturale*. Plus, Pisa.

Dau, F.R (2011) *Costituzionalismo e rappresentanza. Il caso del Sudafrica*. Giuffrè, Milano.

Dau, F.R (2012) The Soul of a Nation: il costituzionalismo sudafricano alla prova della dinamica política. In: Lanchester, F (ed) *La Costituzione degli altri. Dieci anni di trasformazioni in alcuni ordinamenti costituzionali stranieri*. Giuffrè, Milano.

Derrett, J.D.M (1968) *Religion, Law and State in India*. Faber & Faber, London.

Dworkin, R (1978) *Taking Rights Seriously*. Harvard University Press, Cambridge.

100 *Rights in intercultural research*

El Houssi, L (2013) *Il risveglio della democrazia. La Tunisia dall'indipendenza alla transizione*. Carocci, Roma.

Federico, V (2009) *Sudafrica*. Il Mulino, Bologna.

Ghai, Y (ed.) (2000) *Autonomy and Ethnicity: Negotiating Competing Claims in Multi-Ethnic States*. Cambridge University Press, Cambridge.

Glenn, H.P (2013) *The Cosmopolitan State*. Oxford University Press, Oxford.

Gonzáles Galván, J.A (1997) El Estado pluricultural de derecho: los principios y los derechos indígenas constitucionales. *Boletín Mexicano de Derecho Comparado* 88: 169–190.

Goodman, R, Refsing, K (eds) (1992) *Ideology and Practice in Modern Japan*. Routledge, London.

Groppi, T (2011) Il multiculturalismo come strumento per la costruzione dell'identità nazionale: l'esperienza del Canada. In: Amirante, D, Pepe, V (eds) *Stato democratico e società multiculturale. Dalla tutele delle minoranze al riconoscimento delle diversità culturali*. Giappichelli, Torino.

Grosso, E (2006) Multiculturalismo e diritti fondamentali nella Costituzione italiana. In: Bernardi, A (ed) *Multiculturalismo, diritti umani, pena*. Giuffrè, Milano.

Gruzinski, S (1988) *La colonisation de l'imaginaire. Sociétés indigènes et occidentalisation dans le Mexique espagnol. XVIe-XVIIIe siècle*. Gallimard, Paris.

Gutwirth, S, De Hert, P (2010) Regulating Profiling in a Democratic Constitutional State. In: Hildebrandt, M, Gutwirth, S (eds) *Profiling the European Citizen. Cross-Disciplinary Perspectives*. Springer-Verlag, Berlin – Heidelberg.

Häberle, P (1980) Italian edition: (2003) *La dignità umana come fondamento della comunità statale*. In: Id., *Cultura dei diritti e diritti della cultura nello spazio costituzionale europeo*. Saggi, Giuffrè, Milano.

Häberle, P. (2001) *Per una dottrina della costituzione come scienza della cultura*. Carocci, Roma.

Hartmann, N (1949) Etica. Italian edition: Filippone Thaulero, V (1970) *Assiologia dei costumi*, vol. II. Guida Editori, Napoli.

Hughes, A (2014) *Human Dignity and Fundamental Rights in South Africa and Ireland*. Pretoria University Law Press, Pretoria.

Hui, H (2015) *Objectives and Ways of Implementation of the Normative Constitutional School*. In: Levy, K (ed) Commemorating the 30th Anniversary of PRC Constitution, Lit.

Huntington, S.P (1996) The Clash of Civilizations and the Remaking of World Order. Italian edition: (2003) *Lo scontro delle civiltà e il nuovo ordine mondiale*. Garzanti, Milano.

Kant, I (1772) Anthropology from a Pragmatic Point of View. Italian edition: Chiodi, P (ed) (2006) *Antropologia dal punto di vista pragmatico Parte prima. Didattica antropologica. Del modo di conoscere l'interno e l'esterno dell'uomo. Libro I. Della facoltà di conoscere*. In: *Critica della ragion pratica e altri scritti*. Utet, Torino.

Khatib, L (2013) Political Participation and Democratic Transition in the Arab World. *University of Pennsylvania Journal of International Law* 34(29): 315–340.

Kimlycka, W (2005) Liberal Multiculturalism: Western Model, Global Trends and Asian Debates. In: Kimlycka, W, He, B (eds) *Multiculturalism in Asia*. Oxford University Press, Oxford.

Lie, H (2006) The Urgent Task of Establishing the Judicial Review System. In: Buyun, L (ed) *Constitutionalism and China*. Law Press, China.

Lie, H, Xiaoqing, B (2006) *Constitutionalism and China*. Law Press, China.

Lingat, R (2003) *La tradizione giuridica dell'India*. Giuffrè, Milano.

MacDonald, R (1986) Pour la reconnaissance d'une normativité implicite et inférentielle. *Sociologie et sociétés* 18(1).

Mahajan, G (2005) Indian Exceptionalism or Indian Model: Negotiating Cultural Diversity and Minority Rights in a Democratic Nation-State. In: Kimlycka, W, He, B. (eds) *Multiculturalism in Asia*. Oxford University Press, Oxford.

Mahajan, G (2013) *India: Political Ideas and the Making of a Democratic Discourse*. Zed Books, London & New York.

Mahmood, T (1999) Interaction of Islam and Public Law in Independent India. In: Khare, R.S (ed) *Perspectives on Islamic Law, Justice and Society*. Rowman and Littlefield, New York.

Mancini, L (2000) Società multiculturale e diritto italiano. Alcune riflessioni. *Quaderni di diritto e politica ecclesiastica* 1: 71–86.

Mazzarese, T (ed) (2013) *Diritto, tradizioni, traduzioni. La tutela dei diritti nelle società multiculturali*. Giappichelli, Torino.

Menski, W (2006) *Comparative Law in Global Context: The Legal Systems of Asia and Africa*. Cambridge University Press, Cambridge.

Mishra, S, Kumar, B.C (2014) Understanding Diversity: A Multicultural Perspective. *IOSR Journal of Humanities and Social Science (IOSR-JHSS)* 19(9): 62–66.

Moccia, L (2015) The Idea of "Law" in China: An Overview. *European Journal of Sinology* 6.

Morrone, A (2005) Multiculturalismo e Stato costituzionale. In: Vignudelli, A (ed) *Istituzioni e dinamiche del diritto. Multiculturalismo, comunicazione, federalismo*. Einaudi, Torino.

Motta, R (2006) *Riflessioni e aggiornamenti su antropologia giuridica e discipline confinanti*. Trauben, Torino.

Mougnonzo, Esrom Mouel'A (2007) *Coutume, droit et communautarisme. Pour une philosophie du droit africain*. Edilivre, Paris.

Olivetti, M (2013) *Messico*. Il Mulino, Bologna.

Orrù, R (1998) *La Costituzione di tutti: il Sudafrica dalla segregazione razziale alla democrazia della rainbow nation*. Giappichelli, Torino.

Pegoraro, L, Rinella, A (1997) La nuova Costituzione della Repubblica del Sudafrica (1996–1997). *Rivista trimestrale di diritto pubblico* 2.

Perlingieri, P (1972) *La personalità umana nell'ordinamento giuridico*. Jovene, Napoli.

Pinelli, C (2013) Relativismo culturale, scontri di civiltà, costituzionalismo. In: Mazzarese, T (ed) *Diritto, tradizioni, traduzioni. La tutela dei diritti nelle società multiculturali*. Giappichelli, Torino.

Ponthoreau, M.C (2010) *Droit(s) constitutionnel(s) comparé(s). Economica (Corpus Droit public)*. Éditions Economica, Paris.

Quanxi, G (2015) *The Rise of Chinese Political Constitutionalist School*. In: Levy, K (ed) Commemorating the 30th Anniversary of PRC Constitution. Lit.

Rallo Lombarte, A, García Mahamut, R (eds) (2015) *Hacia un nuevo derecho europeo de protección de datos*. Tirant lo Blanch, Valencia.

Rawls, J (1971) Justice as Fairness. Italian edition: (2002) *Giustizia come equità. Una riformulazione*. Feltrinelli, Milano.

Rea Granados, S.A (2015) Derecho a la consulta y la participación de los pueblos indígenas, la experiencia constitucional en los casos de México y Chile. *Boletín Mexicano de Derecho Comparado* 144: 1083–1117.

Resta, G (2000) Revoca del consenso ed interesse al trattamento nella protezione dei dati personali. *Riv. Critica dir. Priv.* 2: 299–333.

Resta, G, Zeno-Zencovich, V (eds) (2015) *Il diritto all'oblio dopo la sentenza Gloogle Spain*. RomaTrE-Press, Roma.

Ricca, V.M (2008) *Dike meticcia. Rotte di diritto interculturale*. Rubbettino, Soveria Mannelli.

Ricca, V.M (2013) *Culture interdette. Modernità, migrazioni, diritto interculturale*. Bollati Boringhieri, Torino.

Ridola, P (2010) *Diritto comparato e diritto costituzionale europeo*. Giappichelli, Torin.

Rohe, M (2006) The Migration and Settlement of Muslims: The Challenges for European Legal Systems. In: Shah, P, Menski, W (eds) *Migration, Diasporas and Legal Systems in Europe*. Routledge, London.

Rouland, N (2002) *Antropologia giuridica*. Giuffrè, Milano.

Rousseau, D (2015) *Radicaliser la démocratie. Propositions pour une refondation*. Seuil, Paris.

Ruggiu, I (2012) *Il giudice antropologo. Costituzione e tecniche di composizione dei conflitti multiculturali*. FrancoAngeli, Milano.

Ruggiu, I (2015) *Dis-eguaglianza e identità culturale: tolleranza e multiculturalismo*. Conference lecture La dis-eguaglianza nello Stato costituzionale, "Gruppo di Pisa", Campobasso June 2015. Available via www.gruppodipisa.it Accessed 16 May 2017.

Sacco, R (2007) *Antropologia giuridica*. Il Mulino, Bologna.

Sacco, R (2009) *Le droit africain. Anthropologie et droit positif*. Dalloz, Paris.

Saraswati, S.N (2002) *Right to Equality in the Indian Constitution. A Gandhian Perspective*. Cocept Publishing Company, New Dehli.

Sartori, G (2000) *Pluralismo, multiculturalismo e estranei. Saggio sulla società multietnica*. Rizzoli, Milano.

Scaffardi, L (1996) La rivoluzionaria tutela dei diritti fondamentali del Sudafrica. *Giurisprudenza costituzionale* 1.

Sen, A (1999) Development as Freedom. Italian edition: (2011) *Globalizzazione e libertà*. Mondadori, Milano.

Sen, A (2006) Democracy Isn't "Western". Italian edition: (2013) *La democrazia degli altri. Perché la libertà non è un'invenzione dell'Occidente*. Mondadori, Milano.

Singh, C (1985) *Law from Anarchy to Utopia*. Oxford University Press, Oxford.

Singh, G, Sharma, R (2015) Human Rights Law in Historical Perspective: Overview of the Human Rights Stances in the Ancient and Medieval India. *Indian Socio-Legal Journal* 1–2.

Strauss, D.A (2009) The Modernizing Mission of Judicial Review. *University of Chicago Law Review* 76.

Twining, W (2000) *Globalization and Legal Theory*. London: Butterworths.

Twining, W (2007) Globalisation and Comparative Law. In Örücü, E, Nelken, D (eds) *Comparative Law: A Handbook*. Hart Publishing, Portland.

Ubertazzi, T.M (2004) *Il diritto alla privacy. Natura e funzioni giuridiche*. Cedam, Padova.

Vasak, K (1982) *The International Dimensions of Human Rights 1*. UNESCO, Praga. Available via http://unesdoc.unesco.org/images/0005/000562/056230Eo.pdf Accessed 16 May 2017.

Warren, S, Brandeis, L (1890) The Right of Privacy. *Harv. L. Rev* 4.

Zagrebelsky, G (2009) *Intorno alla legge. Il diritto come dimensione del vivere comune*. Einaudi, Torino.

5 Law and constitutions as a historical and cultural praxis

5.1 Towards an 'impure' notion of Law. Beyond theoretical and methodological positivism

The contingent and continuously evolving nature of fundamental rights primarily confirms the validity of approaching them through legal, social and human sciences. Such an approach should be reinforced by criticism of the 'pure' notion of law (this notion, based on logical deductions, excludes any reference to individual and social reality from the concept of law).

Previously, an often mistakenly 'natural' and undeniably ideological content of rights has been highlighted, underlining the importance of a legal–historical interpretation of fundamental rights.

However, the attempt to remove the last remaining relics of natural law from traditional legal science is due to Kelsen's Pure Theory of Law[1] and the place where he held his chair and began his teaching: the Vienna School of Legal Thought.

Kelsen's Pure Theory of Law "is a theory of positive law, as a general theory of positive law, concerned with law in general rather than with a specific national or international legal norms, legal orders or their interpretation" (Kelsen 1934, 47).

---

1 Kelsen (1934), in criticizing the ideological character of traditional legal theory, claims the anti-ideological tendency of the Pure Theory of Law. In some of his early writings of the early twentieth century (*Das Verhältnis im Lichte der Erkenntniskritik*, Wien 1921), and later in *Der soziologische und der juristische Staatsbegriff*, Kelsen, by criticizing psychologism and, later, iusnaturalism as foreign elements to legal science, conceives the State as an imaginary personification of the normative complex that constitutes the legal system as a whole. The first Italian scholar who dedicated a critical essay to Kelsen's thought was Condorelli (1923, 307–315), but Frosini (1961/1988, 21–34) and Riccobono (1989) are also worth mentioning. The reaction to Kelsen's formalism of Italian scholars of Public Law culminates in Mortati (1940).

Kelsen systematizes, in both a formal and abstract sense, the purpose of the law in order to purge empirical content or morality and justice values. Nevertheless, this greater 'purity', as a specific purpose of the law, limits both its objective and interpretative scope, given that the choice of conceptual tools derives from the 'rule of law' notion, as seen in Europe. So, where does this demand for 'purity', already manifested in the nineteenth century with Gerber and Laband in Germany, or Orlando in Italy, actually come from?

At the beginning of the 1930s, Kelsen, a remarkable legal theorist, proceeded, during the German democratic defeat, to generalize and further purify his doctrine. In this regard, Renato Treves's (2000, 11) testimony is very significant indeed. In 1932, when Treves met with Kelsen in Cologne, the latter thought that the victory of the National Socialist movement was imminent. Kelsen, a fervent Democrat, had foreseen the consequences of that impending victory and decided to leave Germany and emigrate to another country in order to be able to continue to work freely. Shortly after that rendezvous, Kelsen sent Treves the first draft of one of his unpublished works[2]: *La dottrina pura del diritto. Metodi e concetti fondamentali.* Kelsen had apparently decided that his essay should not only be translated into Italian and other languages, but also be published before publishing it in German.[3]

The 'American' Kelsen,[4] who blossomed from the largely neo-Kantian 'European' one,[5] seemed interested in extending his Pure Theory of Law, which was initially focused on European continental law, to *common law*[6] concepts and institutions. This may well explain why, in the field of legal interpretation, "it was Kelsen who abandoned formalism and began to assume the attitudes of the anti-formalists, denying the legal certainty and affirming that the jurisdictional function is not a declarative but creative function of the Law" (Treves 2000, 17).[7]

The 'pure' notion of law, has validity issues, however. As Heller affirms, it does not know legal validity, or in other words, it knows no concrete,

2 The Italian translation is found in Giuseppe Archivio's 1933 second edition.
3 This eventually happened in 1934 in Vienna, though with a different title.
4 There is even a "final Kelsen", in which "not only empiricism tends to supplant neo-Kantianism, but some earlier theories are radically rejected" (Barberis 2001, 12).
5 This is not a simple Kantian revival, given that Kelsian thought could be observed through Cassier's influence in the early 1920s, at that time, developing his theory of knowledge (Condorelli 1923, Frosini 1988, 23).
6 Hence, as Barberis (2001, 16) affirms, Kelsen transformed pure legal theory into a "general theory/ *general jurisprudence*, even before the *allgemeine Rechtslehre*".
7 Gorla (1941) had already moved away from pure legal science in Italy, claiming the relevance of interpretation.

content-based validity linked to a situation, but it is based more on a "general validity", amounting to no more than "positivism without positivity, a Staatslehre without the state, and a legal science without the law" (Heller 1929, 389). In fact, the validity of the existing rule actually depends on its effectiveness and efficiency (Ross 1958).

'Pure' legal theory, described as inadequate in the first decades of the twentieth century (Schmitt 1928),[8] presupposes a withdrawal of all social and normative references from the law and ends up seizing the 'effectiveness' requirement: 'positivity'. How can norms be attributed a legality that they lack, when they are not observed? One possible answer to this question involves taking a different perspective or, preferably, integrating the legal notion of law.

Institutionalist theories[9] take a prevailing approach which, unlike that of positive legal theory,[10] explains law not in terms of itself, but in terms of its social function.

For this reason, Santi Romano's *institutional* theory of law, as provided for in *L'ordinamento giuridico*,[11] is useful for interpreting different legal systems and analysing both norms and 'normative facts'. In his work, what is 'legal' is not based on logical deductions but rather, is inferred, *ex post*, from *institutions*, i.e. from organizational principles necessary for the preservation of a social group.

Romano's institutionalist view was born out of economic–social pluralist analysis, which permeated his 1909 inaugural lesson[12] in the Faculty of Pisa, *Lo Stato moderno e la sua crisi*, and which provided clarity on early twentieth-century transformations. However, his greatest concern at the time was to assert State unity in the face of the social forces which, in

---

8 However, Schmitt's anti-formalism runs counter to the absolutism of the 'political' autonomy, attributable to the decision 'myth'. This mythification ends up affirming the primacy of the political decision over the legal order's normative element. Smend's analysis, which strives to overcome the dualism that characterizes Jellinek's State theory, and also Kelsen's normativism, conceives the State as "integration", which is interesting, especially after its successive developments (i.e. as a process of lasting union between persons). The possible forms that the State could adopt would depend on the "types of integration systems" envisioned (Smend 1928).

9 For the most significant French institutionalist theories, see Hauriou (1925, 2–45) and his disciple, Renard (1930).

10 See Bobbio (1962).

11 The work was published between 1917 and 1918, in two successive numbers of the *Annali delle Università toscane* and in a volume published in Pisa in 1918. The 1951 second edition, Firenze, is cited here.

12 This was published in 1910 in *Rivista di diritto pubblico*. There are many contributions made on Santi Romano's work.

his opinion, should be reincorporated as part of the State. Thus, in this opening lesson, Romano's integrationist ideology is still highlighted, whereas in
his work *L'ordinamento giuridico*, a pluralistic theoretical stance prevails,
and the fact of social and institutional conflict, as essential features of the
modern State are generally assumed.

In the institutional theory of law, Romano overcomes the state-centric
notion of law. In particular, he criticizes the monopoly for normative production, in the form of acts, with the aim of giving greater theoretical content to his pluralist theses. His opening pluralistic theory of legal systems,
derived from the joint essential nature of society and law, does not deter-
mine any hierarchy among various institutions.[13] After the advent of Fascism, Romano defines the State as the original, sole, and sovereign legal
system; ideologically, he can be qualified as 'monist'[14] despite being, in
theory, a 'pluralist'.

Romano's legal considerations do not have a perfect or linear logic: he
seems to come to the conclusion that historical events do not allow for
pluralistic premises. After the Fascist regime, the essays contained in his
final work,[15] published in 1947,[16] seem more closely aligned to his work
L'ordinamento giuridico. Of course, in this new *context*, Santi Romano's
institutionalist approach to the principle of plurality of legal systems awak-
ens a renewed interest in Italy.

References to institutionalist theory in Santi Romano's work are by no
means incidental, since references to different *contexts* and *social pluralism*
are very useful, especially in multicultural societies. This is so in terms of
understanding different agents and problems which require new standards
or, at least, standards that allow for different meanings by virtue of their
evolutionary interpretation.

For this very reason, it seems appropriate to reconsider the positive
aspects of institutionalist theories. At the same time, emphasizing the

---

13 The latter is confirmed by Orlando's (1924/1954, 326) critique of Romano's theory. He
asked, in defence of traditional theory, whether the theory of plurality of legal systems was
compatible with the principle of the sovereignty of the modern State.

14 Bobbio has accurately characterized Romano's (1977, 43) monism as a "relative monism",
for "although he placed the State at the top of the hierarchy, as superior to the social order,
he did not consider it an exclusive one". Also see Cassese and Azzariti, in general, and
Fotia, (2011, 167), Morrone (2012, 369) and Martinelli (2014) in particular.

15 *Frammenti di un dizionario giuridico*, which contains some essays written between 1944
and 1946. See also the new edition of the 1983 original (Giuffrè, Milan) with Alberto
Romano's *Presentation*.

16 This was the year in which he passed away.

positivity of constitutionally[17] enshrined principles, within a framework of legal reflection, might also prove useful. It is in this way that the concept of institution, from a legal point of view, does not disintegrate into a "liquid society", where economic organizational principles prevail, due to the advances of a global economy.

These critical considerations on theoretical positivism can be extrapolated to methodological positivism, which adopts a neutral axiological view of legal theory. Cognitive relativism and legal comparison,[18] on the contrary, do not exclude value judgements about legal facts – nor do they necessarily presuppose an ethically neutral stance. The only 'neutrality' presumed is that which professes equal dignity for all cultures. This does not preclude value judgements but rather, cultural discrimination on the various human rights cultures.

Criticism of the limits of methodological and theoretical positivism does not require a return to 'natural law theory' but rather, a revision of one's own understanding of law and its application, for it is often reduced to a mere logical/deductive activity. If methodological positivism is the theory in which the act of describing the law as it is (and not judging how it *should* be) belongs to legal science, then an axiological perspective cannot be ruled out. From this perspective, fundamental values have been historically objectified in society and in law, and recognized and confirmed as constitutionally enshrined, fundamental principles.

For this reason, fundamental principles of a particular legal order are *different* but not *foreign* to the values upon which they are built. Thus, constitutional principles are neither 'true' nor 'fair': they are legally relevant because shared by society in a particular moment in history and, as such, are subject to review by legal interpreter-practitioners. This way, the inclusion of an axiological perspective is not confused with an ideological one. This latter value therefore, joins with legal formalism and the state-centric notion of the law and rights (understood merely as products of the sovereign power's self-limitation).

17 Note that the normativity of constitutional principles is useful even to guard against the empirical determination of the legal phenomenon being taken to extremes. This would result in theorizing about a kind of interpretive realism based on the unreal contrast between interpretation as an act of will, and interpretation as an act of knowledge. According to Michel Troper (1994 and 2001), a norm is a decision that is created by legally imposing bodies responsible for its authentic interpretation. It is not only a theory of legal interpretation, but also a general theory of law that considers it as a set of empirical facts. Also the confrontation between Troper and Pfersmann, might be of particular interest. The latter is very critical of Troper's theories; see Pfersmann and Troper (2007).

18 We speak of law, not of 'laws', because we only knew our respective national law at first. For this reason, the other foreign legal orders are mentioned marginally (Moréteau 2009, 699).

On the other hand, a useful contribution to legal theory comes from legal positivism critics, who comprehend law as a "historical-cultural experience"[19] and, also from 'neo-constitutionalist' critics who, in objecting to positivism, apply a deep, critical revision of the rupture, caused by positivism itself, between law and morality.[20] In addition, the more moderate schools of legal positivism[21] have helped to strengthen legal categories, not by rejecting the positive law assessment, but rather by including moral issues in legal discourse (*Inclusive Legal Positivism*).[22]

This interest in value elements should not lead to a partial reading of legal institutions. To a greater extent, the inclusion of legal institutions in legal comparison, so as to avoid a distorting effect, requires full awareness of cultural relativity on the part of the scholar.

Legal comparison presupposes relativization and is useful for that very reason. For comparative scholars, socio-cultural contextualization of normative data is essential: only in this way are legal institutions comprehensible in space and in time. If, on the contrary, comparative methods are limited to the collection of normative data, the resulting analysis will lack contextualization. In other words, it will entirely lack the historical-cultural evolution of relevant legal institutions, and so miss vital relevant concepts. If this methodological problem is ignored, interpretation of other legal experiences can only be superficial and compromise the main (cognitive) purpose of the researcher of comparative law.

5.2 Meaning and functions of the notion of "cross-cultural constitutionalism"

Along with cultural and institutional pluralism, which develops out of a social context, understood in a conflicting and dynamic way, the search for new notions to make State, intercultural fundamental rights and

---

19 For a critique on legal positivism, reference must also be made to Miguel Reale. For him, law is a "historical-cultural experience" and, therefore, is presented as a "three-dimensional" unit: "norm", "value" and "fact". Hence, according to Reale (1953/1956, 1968a/1968b/1973), an authentic "legal" knowledge cannot exist without axiological and factual elements. In Italy, this has been thoroughly analyzed by Capograssi (1937). On this subject, see also Galizia (2003, 395). In the early 1950s, contributions to legal science made through historical research are striking. Some of Orestano's studies (1959, 785–829; 1960, 149–196), which show how concepts change their meaning dependent on historical events, are especially relevant.
20 See Dworkin (1977), Alexy (1992, 1998), Zagrebelsky (1992) and Baldassarre (2007, 3276).
21 See Hart (1961/2002).
22 This legal school of thought developed in the United States during the 1920s. See, among others, Waluchow (1994) and Pace (2007, 83).

110   *Rights in intercultural research*

constitutional theory contributions continues apace. The most rewarding way forward is to consider the relationship between international, universal and regional law, as well as national law itself.[23]

The concept of *cross-cultural constitutionalism* presents itself not only (as we will see) as a hermeneutic requirement of the legal phenomenon[24] but also, and even earlier, as a familiar approach to comparative scholars, who are attentive to diversity and mindful of cultural and institutional contaminations. Objectively speaking, *cross-cultural constitutionalism* is a *historical-cultural fact*: it manifests itself as a legal language with essentially universal connotations, yet it is empirically focused on the sociocultural contextualization of normative data. Indeed, everything that is legally relevant, and which appears in legal theories, must also apply to behaviours, actions, (general) principles or shared norms (*de facto*, all of these rules and norms constitute what we refer to as the law).

From this broad concept, *cross-cultural constitutionalism* assumes the features of a constitutional metacode based not on abstract principles but on general principles of law. These general principles influence the production of norms, and are eventually constitutionally enshrined, becoming positive law elements. In contrast with traditional provisions of positivist legal discourse, such general principles are not only a programmatic supralegal repertoire, but also possess a prescriptive-normative character, thanks to an approach consolidated during the second half of the twentieth century in the works of Crisafulli (1941, 1952), Esser (1972) and Larenz (1960).

Moreover, general principles supersede positive law, undermining their development when they are presented as 'open' rules to social elements that represent the fruitful life of the law. This approach allows us to recognize the intertwined character of the relationship between general principles of law and constitutional principles, in the sense that, even in the notion of 'cross-cultural constitutionalism', they corroborate each other.

Cross-constitutionalism therefore requires legal research which focuses on identifying general principles common to and present in different systems, along with positive historical events, insofar as their degree of *consensus* can be legally confirmed (the basis of constitutional systems will be considered here, along with their rigidity and stability). Thus, *consensus*, in terms of legal terminology, has a universalist connotation, as it constitutes the basis of each norm in relation to the recognition of human dignity, the respect and recognition of *others* (naturally similar) and of the (other

---

23 These relations are even more complex, taking into account EU law.
24 See Betti (1962), Gadamer (1960), Mohr (1922), Esser (1972) and Viola and Zaccaria (2004).

culturally diverse) *similar*. This respect and recognition must be confirmed by general principles of the legal order in question, beginning with its constitutional enshrinement (positivisation).

Effective consensus can be achieved only when cultural pluralism allows for democratic multiculturalism and for an open, active and inclusive citizenship, capable of simultaneously assessing rights and duties in its historical and logical correlation[25] at a legal-constitutional level.[26] This cannot, however, be in absolute terms[27] – legally recognized rights will sometimes prove inadequate.[28] Without aiming to reduce fundamental rights language to its functional, specific legal dictates, it is useful to maintain a certain correlation between them, for rights and duties cannot be exercised without an overall sense of their meaning. Why are some rights fundamental or superior to the rest? How can they be effectively protected? How can we specifically guarantee them?

There is no answer to these questions, unless constitutionalism and constitutional theory are endowed with internal principles and norms that define and establish priorities. Sadly, every fundamental rights theory must take these steps so that, in fact, citizenship can take shape. Without the 'right to have rights', authoritarianism and/or paternalism would reign. Equally, without the 'obligation to have obligations', individual egos, privileges and inequalities would hold sway.

The notion of cross-cultural constitutionalism not only recognizes but also actually places value on this process of norming character rights and duties.

One of the main functions of *cross-cultural constitutionalism* is to foster a dialogue between different cultures. For example, Eastern cultures have a somewhat contrary position with respect to the recognition of human rights according to a individualistic conception born and raised in the Western systems. Fortunately, post–World War II democratic constitutions, and even earlier constitutions such as Weimar (1919) and Mexico (1917), internalized and surpassed this purely individualistic conception, beginning with the recognition of social rights.

---

25 See Hohfeld (1923), Aldershot (2001), Hart (1954), Steiner (1994, 74) and Bobbio (2014, 19).

26 It is worth mentioning some Italian works whereby special attention was given to the subject of constitutional duties: Lombardi (1967), Pezzini and Sacchetto (2005), Florenzano Re, et al. (2015), Grandi (2014).

27 After the 1960s, Hart (1961) did not exclude the possibility that there were rights which did not correlate with duties.

28 The absence of correlative obligations and prohibitions does not imply the absence of fundamental rights, if an obligation to introduce is at least present (Ferrajoli 2007, 675).

This approach to fundamental rights (and duties) requires caution and must be taken on board with a certain scepticism, in order to ensure the effectiveness of rights in a universal dimension,[29] as if a kind of cosmopolitan constitutionalism, or a constitutionalism of international law were possible (Habermas 2006, 107).

However, a consideration of legal language within universal connotations has its place, for it can help reaffirm imported principles of modern and democratic constitutionalism and also identify new principles that involve distinct good practices and values to apply to markets.

Affirming an ethics of principles which, following the ideas of Weber, makes principles absolute, unrenounceable and fair on their own, is not the intention here. Not only is cross-cultural constitutionalism both a way of thinking and a cultural event (originating from the contamination and circulation of constitutional models), but it is also a *constitutionalism of general principles of law*. This is the case when it incorporates, in legal language, principles and norms that, though not assumed nor admitted in absolute terms, are verifiable, shared and placed as the basis of a plurality of constitutional systems, precisely by virtue of their *management capacity*. Hence, general principles derive from reality (Gény 1899) and, in particular, from the social forces that have influenced their 'materialisation'. These principles can be extrapolated into multiple and different legal orders, not only because they are not abstract in nature, being derived from the circulation and contamination of legal systems as well as specific cultures, but also because of their verifiable normative 'force' (which, in turn, is different in every particular normative context).

There is another aspect that guides this work: individualized and verifiable normative principles must be understood as limits to power and as a guarantee of fundamental rights. It is for this very reason that constitutional theory can only remain anchored in constitutionalism's historical roots, even during intercultural research on fundamental rights.

From a theoretical point of view, *cross-cultural constitutionalism* can be used as a *hermeneutic category* of legal phenomena, which projects pluralism over concrete dimensions of the law with intercultural connotations. This has a vital argumentative function with respect to constitutional theories which, on the one hand, have lost modern and contemporary constitutional principles and on the other, are incapable of developing new, useful

---

29 Rodotà (2014, 71) points to a more optimistic attitude, in favour of the creation of a "global community of courts", associated with the protection of rights, and also "initiatives that, starting with civil society and having as reference international documents, manage to carry out guarantees".

legal categories in order to recognize and interpret constitutional changes and new-found social conflicts.

From a methodological point of view, this suggested category can be used to show the limits of a useless, redundant pursuit of 'purity' within the context of legal methods, a search that constitutes an obstacle to the spatial and temporal understanding of legal phenomena.

Instead, it is worth emphasizing the importance of interpreting rights, norms, case law and legal principles without resorting to generic concepts,[30] but rather by examining at specific problems and inter-subjective relationships linked to different contexts. This is a foreign approach within many legal theories and is understood as false consciousness. It is an approach which seeks to value the historical-legal matrix of fundamental rights: it is also one which establishes cultural autonomy vis-à-vis law over power and economy, whilst recognizing the inevitable influence of politically relevant social forces on the law.

Cross-cultural constitutionalism specifically appears as a *hermeneutic* category of cultural and institutional pluralism, which inevitably manifests itself as the conflictual profile of social dynamics. For this reason, general enshrined (positivized) principles *must* have regulatory capacity – a higher normative, or in other words, *constitutional* 'force'. Always, these enshrined principles must also have the fullest respect for pluralism, which takes legal form to recognize and protect individual, collective and community rights.

Cross-cultural constitutionalism, in its global reach, refers to the interpretation of universally inclusive general principles of law, which cannot be reduced to a given context. Nevertheless, these principles need definition in order to be effectively protected, and are, therefore, in need of a link with 'positive' (normative) reality.

In this light, *cross-cultural constitutionalism* acts from a classical constitutional stance in distancing itself from global economy constitutionalism that turns citizens into mere consumers.[31] Finally, cross-cultural constitutionalism integrates the liberal multicultural perspective, which is strongly anchored in individual rights, and democratic multiculturalism, which instead values cultural and social differences within a united political-institutional organization and constitutional framework, beginning with its *principles*.

---

30 In relation to this philosophical aspect, see Della Volpe (1942), and prior to his approach to Marxism (between 1943 and 1944) must be highlighted. Similarly, see Della Volpe (1950, 1956) with some modifications and an annex with a "logical positivism critique".
31 On the other hand, consumer consent cannot be fully and knowingly understood where will is compromised by a vitiating factor: a position of weakness, subordination or any other form of dependence.

References

Alexy, R (1992) *Concetto e validità del diritto*. Giuffrè, Milano.

Alexy, R (1998) *Teoria dell'argomentazione giuridica*. Giuffrè, Milano.

Baldassarre, A (2007) Una risposta a Guastini. *Giur. Cost.* 4: 3276 and following.

Barberis, M (2001) Introduzione. In: Kelsen, H (ed) *La democracia*. Il Mulino, Bologna.

Betti, E (1962) *L'ermeneutica come metodica generale delle scienze dello spirito*. Città Nuova, Roma.

Bobbio, N (1962) Giusnaturalismo e positivismo giuridico. *Rivista di diritto civile* 6.

Bobbio, N (1977) Teoria e ideologia nella dottrina di Santi Romano. In: Biscaretti de Ruffia, P (ed) *Le dottrine giuridiche di oggi e l'insegnamento di Santi Romano*. Giuffrè, Milano.

Bobbio, N (2014) Introduzione. In: *L'età dei diritti*. Einaudi, Torino.

Condorelli, O (1923) Il rapporto tra Stato e diritto secondo Kelsen. *Rivista internazionale di filosofia del diritto* 3: 307–315.

Crisafulli, V (1941) Per la determinazione del concetto dei principî generali del diritto. *Rivista internazionale di filosofia del diritto*, 1–2: 41–63, 3: 157–181, 4–5: 230–264.

Crisafulli, V (1952) *La Costituzione e le sue disposizioni di principio*. Giuffrè, Milano.

Della Volpe, G (1942) *Critica dei principi logici*. D'Anna, Messina.

Dworkin, R (1977) *Taking Rights Seriously*. Available via http://philosophyfaculty. ucsd.edu/faculty/rarneson/DWORKINTakingRightsSeriously.pdf Accessed 16 May 2017.

Esser, J (1972) Vorverständnis und Methodenwahl in der Rechtsfindung. Italian edition: (1983) *Precomprensione e scelta del metodo nel processo di individuazione del diritto. Fondamenti di razionalità nella prassi decisionale del giudice* (trans Patti, S, Zaccaria, G). Edizioni Scientifiche Italiane, Napoli.

Ferrajoli, L (2007) *Principia iuris. Teoria del diritto e della democrazia. I. Teoria del diritto*. Laterza, Roma-Bari.

Florenzano, D, Borgonovo Re, G, Cortese, F (2015) *Diritti fondamentali, doveri di solidarietà e principio di eguaglianza: un'introduzione*. Giappichelli, Torino.

Fotia, M (2011) L'istituzionalismo in Santi Romano tra Diritto e Politica. *Democrazia e diritto* 1–2.

Frosini, V (1961) La critica italiana a Kelsen. *Rivista internazionale di filosofia del diritto* 38.

Frosini, V (1988) *Saggi su Kelsen e Capograssi. Due interpretazioni del diritto*. Giuffrè, Milano.

Gadamer, H.G (1960) Wahrheit und Methode. Grundzüge einer philosophischen Hermeneutik. Italian edition: (2000) *Verità e metodo* (trans Vattimo, G). Bompiani, Milano.

Galizia, M (2003) Esperienza giuridica Libertà Costituzione. Ricordi di Giuseppe Capograssi, maestro di diritto e di cattolicesimo liberale. *Il Politico* 3: 395 and following.

Gény, F (1899) *Méthode d'interprétation et sources en droit privé positif*. Second edition (1919). LGDJ, Paris.

Gorla, G (1941) *L'interpretazione del diritto*. Giuffrè, Milano.

Grandi, F (2014) *Doveri costituzionali e obiezione di coscienza*. Editoriale Scientifica, Napoli.

Habermas, J (2006) Does the Constitutionalization of International Law Still Have a Chance? Italian edition: *La costituzionalizzazione del diritto internazionale ha ancora una possibilità?* In: Id., *L'Occidente diviso* (trans Carpitella, M). Laterza, Roma-Bari.

Hart, H.L.A (1954) Definition and Theory in Jurisprudence. *Law Quarterly Review*. Italian edition: *Definizione e teoria nella giurisprudenza*. In: Frosini, V (ed) (1964) *Contributi all'analisi del diritto*. Giuffrè, Milano.

Hart, H.L.A. (1961) The Concept of Law. Italian edition: (2002) *Il concetto di diritto*. Einaudi, Torino.

Hauriou, M (1925) La théorie de l'institution et de la fondation. *Cahiers de la Nouvelle Journée* 4: 2–45.

Heller, H (1929) Osservazioni sulla problematica attuale della teoria dello Stato e del diritto. In: Pasquino, P, Kelsen, H (ed) (1987) *La sovranità ed altri scritti sulla dottrina del diritto e dello Stato*. Giuffrè, Milano.

Hohfeld, W. N (1923) Fundamental Legal Conceptions as Applied in Judicial Reasoning. Italian edition: (1969) *Concetti giuridici fondamentali*. Einaudi, Torino.

Kelsen, H (1934). Italian edition: (2000) *Lineamenti di dottrina pura del diritto*. Einaudi, Torino.

Larenz, K (1960) Methodenlehre Der Rechtswissenschaft. Italian edition: (1970) *Storia del metodo nella scienza giuridica, in civiltà del diritto*. Giuffrè, Milano.

Lombardi, G (1967) *Contributo allo studio dei doveri costituzionali*. Giuffrè, Milano.

Martinelli, C (2014) Lo Stato e le fonti del diritto: spunti di riflessione sul pensiero di Santi Romano. *Diritto Amministrativo* 4.

Mohr, J.C (1922) Das Verhältnis im Lichte der Erkenntniskritik. Italian edition: (1995) *Il concetto sociologico e il concetto giuridico dello Stato*. E.S.I., Napoli.

Moréteau, O (2009) Les frontières de la langue et du droit: vers une méthodologie de la traduction juridique. *Revue internationale de droit comparé* 4.

Morrone, A (2012) Per il metodo del costituzionalista: riflettendo su "Lo Stato moderno e la sua crisi" di Santi Romano. *Quaderni costituzionali* 2: 369 and following.

Orestano, R (1959) Azione. In: *Enciclopedia del diritto* Vol. IV. Giuffrè, Milano, pp. 785–829.

Orestano, R (1960) Diritti soggettivi e diritti senza soggetto. *Jus* 11: 149–196.

Orlando, V.E (1954) Lo Stato sindacale nella letteratura giuridica contemporánea. In: Orlando, V.E (ed) *Diritto pubblico generale. Scritti varii (1881–1940)*. Giuffrè, Milano.

Pace, A (2007) Interpretazione costituzionale e interpretazione per valori. In: Azzariti, G (ed) *Interpretazione costituzionale*. Giappichelli, Torino.

Pezzini, B, Sacchetto, C (eds) (2005) *Il dovere di solidarietà*. Giuffrè, Milano.

Pfersmann, O, Troper, M, Omaggio, V (eds) (2007) *Dibattito sulla teoria realistica dell'interpretazione*. Editoriale scientifica, Napoli.

Reale, M (1953) *Filosofia do direito*. São Paulo. Italian edition: (1956) *Filosofia del diritto*. Giappichelli, Torino.

Reale, M (1968a) *O dereito como esperiencia*. São Paulo. Italian edition: (1973) *Il diritto come esperienza*. Giuffrè, Milano.

Reale, M (1968b) *Teoria Tridimensional do Direito*. Edição Saraiva, São Paulo.

Renard, G (1930) *Théorie de l'institution: essai d'ontologie juridique*. Librairie du Recueil Sirey, Paris.

Riccobono, F (1989) *Interpretazioni kelseniane*. Milano, Giuffrè.

Rodotà, S (2014) *Solidarietà*. Un'utopia necessaria, Roma-Bari.

Ross, A (1958) *On Law and Justice*. London. Italian edition: Gavazzi, G (ed) (1965) *Diritto e giustizia*. Einaudi, Torino.

Schmitt, C (1928) *Verfassungslehre*. Berlin. Italian edition: (1984) *Dottrina della costituzione*. Giuffrè, Milano.

Smend, R (1928) Constitution and Constitutional. Italian edition: (1988) *Costituzione e diritto costituzionale*. Giuffrè, Milano.

Steiner, H (1994) *An Essay on Rights*. Blackwell, Oxford.

Treves, R (2000) Prefazione. In: Kelsen, H (ed) *Lineamenti di dottrina pura del diritto*. Einaudi, Torino.

Viola, F, Zaccaria, G (2004) *Diritto e interpretazione. Lineamenti di teoria ermeneutica del diritto*. Laterza, Roma-Bari.

Waluchow, W.J (1994) *Inclusive Legal Positivism*. Clarendon Press, Oxford.

Zagrebelsky, G (1992) *Il diritto mite*. Einaudi, Torino.

Index

120   *Index*

122   *Index*

For Product Safety Concerns and Information please contact our
EU representative GPSR@taylorandfrancis.com Taylor & Francis
Verlag GmbH, Kaufingerstraße 24, 80331 München, Germany